Passover:

The Key That Unlocks the Book of Revelation

Passover:
The Key That Unlocks the Book of Revelation

Daniel C. Juster, Th.D.

With Foreword by Asher Intrater

Lederer Books
A division of
Messianic Jewish Publishers
Clarksville, MD 21029

ISBN 13: 978-1-936716-21-0
Library of Congress Control Number: 2011924079

Cover by M. Hurley
Page Design and Layout Yvonne Vermillion

2015   3

First published in 1991 as Revelation: The Passover Key

Published by:
Lederer Books
A Division of Messianic Jewish Publishers
6120 Day Long Lane
Clarksville, MD 21029

Distributed by:
Messianic Jewish Resources Int'l.
Order line: (800) 410-7367
Lederer@messianicjewish.net
www.messianicjewish.net

Use above contact information to obtain
quantity discounts for resale, bible study groups or other purposes.

Printed in the United States of America

Contents

Foreword

Dan Juster's insights into the Book of Revelation offer several advantages to the reader. First, Dan is a widely read scholar, who is well versed in many streams of Church thought and theology. When he explains a text from Revelation, he is taking into consideration the various ways the text has been interpreted throughout history. This gives the reader the benefit of a *broad-based analysis* without having to do all of the background research.

Second, Dan uses the story of the Passover as a key to understanding the highly symbolic and complicated language of the Book of Revelation. The comparisons of Pharaoh with the Anti-Messiah, the plagues of Exodus with the plagues of Revelation, and the Red Sea victory with Armageddon—among others—help to simplify and make sense of the overall meaning of the End Times prophecies. The application of Old Testament symbolism to Revelation is the correct approach to understanding the book's symbolism.

Finally, Dan's experience as a pastor leads him to draw practical applications from the Book of Revelation that will help believers live by faith in these End Times. Ultimately, the Passover led to great victory for God's people, and in the same way the events of the Book of Revelation will culminate in the manifestation of God's Kingdom on earth. Just as the Israelites in Goshen were protected from the plagues, so the faithful saints of the End Times will be sealed and protected by God's power.

Dan's unique combination of scholarship, messianic theology, and practical pastoring provides a perspective on the Book of Revelation that is truly eye opening. It will help to prepare you for Yeshua's imminent return. Read and enjoy.

Asher Intrater
Director of Revive Israel
Jerusalem, Israel

Preface

Since the publication of the first edition of this book, my convictions have been strengthened. I believe that the basic thrust of the book is correct. This edition will support the interpretation with numerous references. Those who are of a more scholarly bent will benefit from the footnotes, quotations, and summaries of text references.

I have been especially encouraged by the writings of Richard Bauckham on the Book of Revelation. He gives strong support for most of my symbolic references connected to Passover and Exodus. There are some basic variations in our interpretations; Bauckham leans more toward the preterist and symbolic interpretations, meaning this book mostly has reference to the first century but holds the symbolic content is valuable in spiritual warfare at all times. My view that Revelation will be the most relevant to the generation alive when Yeshua returns, of course, is not in accord with his view. My view is more futurist perspective, which will become clear in the text. However, he does hold that in Revelation the ultimate victory after persecution refers to the very end of this age, so we are not so far apart on that account.

In addition, I think it is important to note that although Bauckham and others give strong support for the symbolic interpretations of Passover and Exodus being replicated on a worldwide scale, none has seen Revelation's whole progression as matching the progression of events in Passover and Exodus. This insight might be the Lord's prophetic application or the author's intended pattern of Revelation. When all of the symbolic identifications by individual scholars are put together, it is a bit surprising that no one has indicated the parallel between Exodus and Revelation in the overall pattern of events. I hope that this new edition is a great encouragement.

Introduction

This book is intended to be a general introduction to the Book of Revelation. It does not pretend to be an exhaustive interpretive commentary. It is not my purpose to interpret each verse or to identify every symbol, event, and numerical prediction. It is rather my intent to provide a key that will open up a broad, inspiring, and practical understanding of the book.

The Uniqueness of Revelation

The Book of Revelation is usually understood as an example of the genre of apocalyptic literature. Unfortunately, a survey of scholars who use the term *apocalyptic* shows that its definition varies greatly among scholars. The word itself comes from the Greek meaning "to reveal" or "to unveil." However, the broader view—of showing the unseen world and its effect on the seen world—is not sufficiently precise. The Bible is full of the breaking in of the unseen. Should the Sinai event be categorized as apocalyptic? In this most broad context, it would be, but again that definition is too broad. I use the term in agreement with those scholars who look for the following features: a revelation of the unseen world impinging on this world, highly symbolic language and pictures, and an emphasis on events of the end of days or the end of this age. Texts in the Hebrew Scriptures such as Exodus 19 and 20, Daniel, Ezekiel 38 and 39, or Joel 3 would be early examples of this literature. There are other examples from the Second Temple period.

However, Revelation is a unique work, and no other piece of literature puts together the theme, the progression of events, and the victory of Yeshua in comparable ways. The logical progression of the events described in Revelation can be diagrammed according to seals, trumpets, and bowls of wrath that show the basic progression of the book. Included in the chart below are parenthetical notes that either give a more detailed symbolic picture of the meaning of events or may give a picture that covers the history of God's people.

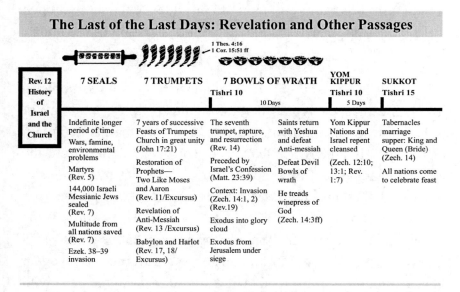

The Last of the Last Days: Revelation and Other Passages

Rev. 12 History of Israel and the Church	7 SEALS	7 TRUMPETS	7 BOWLS OF WRATH Tishri 10		YOM KIPPUR Tishri 10	SUKKOT Tishri 15
				10 Days	5 Days	
	Indefinite longer period of time	7 years of successive Feasts of Trumpets Church in great unity (John 17:21)	The seventh trumpet, rapture, and resurrection (Rev. 14)	Saints return with Yeshua and defeat Anti-messiah	Yom Kippur Nations and Israel repent cleansed	Tabernacles marriage supper: King and Queen (Bride) (Zech. 14)
	Wars, famine, environmental problems	Restoration of Prophets— Two Like Moses and Aaron (Rev. 11/Excursus)	Preceded by Israel's Confession (Matt. 23:39)	Defeat Devil Bowls of wrath	(Zech. 12:10; 13:1; Rev. 1:7)	All nations come to celebrate feast
	Martyrs (Rev. 5)		Context: Invasion (Zech. 14:1, 2) (Rev.19)	He treads winepress of God (Zech. 14:3ff)		
	144,000 Israeli Messianic Jews sealed (Rev. 7)	Revelation of Anti-Messiah (Rev. 13 /Excursus)	Exodus into glory cloud			
	Multitude from all nations saved (Rev. 7)	Babylon and Harlot (Rev. 17, 18/ Excursus)	Exodus from Jerusalem under siege			
	Ezek. 38–39 invasion					

Note that the timeline of the events doesn't match the way Revelation is organized as a book. In the same way, my approach to discussing Revelation will follow the timeline of events and not the order in which the book is written.

A Matter of Interpretation

The Book of Revelation's particulars can be interpreted in a variety of ways. Some of these variations are compatible interpretations and applications; others are ultimately incompatible. Some are convincing; others are farfetched. I believe that the Passover–Exodus key to the Book of Revelation provides us with the best overall understanding for evaluating various approaches.

The Book of Revelation also is notoriously difficult to interpret. A few years ago, the late dean of the graduate school at Wheaton College, Dr. Merrill Tenney, published a book entitled *Interpreting Revelation*. This is a very fine work for a student who wishes to gain a better grasp of Revelation. I believe most interpretations of Revelation use one or a combination of the following approaches outlined in Dr. Tenney's book:

The Symbolic Approach

This approach looks primarily to gain insight into the nature of spiritual opposition and struggle at all times and for all believers. Through this method, all believers undergoing persecution or duress can be encouraged by the ultimate victory of Yeshua and his Kingdom. Those of this school shun historical or prophetic past or future identifications for the book's symbols and content.

Augustine was the most famous interpreter of the symbolic school. The famous fourth-century mystic and theologian saw Revelation as repeating seven cycles with varying terms. Each cycle shows the nature of spiritual warfare during the current age and ends with Yeshua's reign. Hence, the seals, trumpets, and bowls of wrath cover the same time period. The millennium of Revelation 20 also covers that same period.

The symbolic approach recognizes that Revelation is to have immediate relevance to the spiritual struggle of the persecuted Church in any age. All interpreters recognize that the book is full of symbol and metaphor. However, this school shuns ties to specific past, present, and future events so that believers of any time might see themselves in the spiritual warfare presented. Every generation is to see themselves as perhaps the last generation before Yeshua returns. Some who represent the symbolic approach believe that the book will seem most awesomely true for the last generation of this transitional age. I believe that this interpretation is very important and provides true application for believers, especially those under great trials. This is the approach taken by Richard Bauckham and several of the books I use as references.

The Preterist Approach

This views the book as presenting the spiritual struggle of the first-century believers with the Roman Empire and non-Messianic Jewish opposition. It is believed that the prophetic content of the book is fully in the past, except for the literal return of Yeshua the Messiah. The preterist approach is important because it calls us to fully see the background of the book. Certainly the worship-demanding Roman emperor was an anti-Messiah. The book's seven hills unmistakably point to the Seven Hills of Rome. I believe John's prophecy made more sense to last first- and early second-century believers than to any other generation in history.[1]

---

1. I believe Revelation will have more immediate meaning for those just before the Second Coming. It will be more appropriate for them than even the first-century community. The people of God in the Last Days will find themselves in a situation that most closely parallels that of the early Church.

The Historical Approach

This perspective looks at the book as representing the historical progress from the time of Yeshua the Messiah's Ascension until his Second Coming and the establishment of the New Jerusalem. Days and calculations in the book are seen as symbolic of years. The historical approach shows that throughout history there have been many situations that parallel Revelation's content. It also gives a vivid sense that we are closer to the Lord's arrival than any previous generation, mostly because the book progresses to the climax of the Second Coming and because the crisis events of history seem more and more potentially devastating on a world level.

For example, the Reformers after Luther saw Revelation in historical terms. They saw the pope himself as the clearest revelation of the Anti-Messiah. They identified the plagues and struggles in the book as connected to historical events.

Some combine the historical tradition with the preterist persuasion. This is especially so for those who believe that the Church will conquer all obstacles and rule the whole world for a thousand years (Rev. 20) before Yeshua the Messiah returns. Thus, they do not necessarily expect a future anti-Messiah to arise. Indeed, the Olivet Discourse of Matthew 24, Luke 21, and Mark 13 are all seen as referring to first-century events; most of Revelation is seen as having occurred during the Roman Empire.

The Futurist Approach

The fourth way to look at the book, especially after Revelation 4, is as representing the Great Tribulation before the return of Yeshua. While the futurist might credit the value of the other approaches as an encouragement for believers, he sees the ultimate and best application as referring to the events at the end of the age just before the return of the Lord.

As will be seen throughout this book, my approach, though having sympathy with some of the features of each approach, is most oriented toward the futurist. I do believe that parts of Revelation span this entire age. However, I believe that some parts will find their greatest fulfillment in events yet to take place upon the earth. The seals seem capable of applying to many periods of history. However, the trumpet period and the bowls of wrath that follow are more specific and in many regards are more difficult to apply to past history. These texts appear to be symbolic descriptions of events shortly before the literal return of Yeshua.

There is significant truth in each of the four approaches to the Book of Revelation. Rare is the teacher who does not teach his view dogmatically. A student of the Word can be shaken as he hears one forceful presentation after another but finds them to be contradictory. It's important to know that each of these interpretations contains some truth.

Theological Persuasion and Interpretation

These interpretive approaches to Revelation are used by people of widely differing theological persuasions: premillennial, amillennial, and postmillennial. These terms have been used to define what different scholars believe about the timeline of events in Revelation.

Premillennialists believe that a literal thousand-year messianic millennial age of peace on earth (Rev. 20) precedes the full establishment of the new heaven and earth. This thousand-year reign will be when believers of this current age will reign with the Messiah in resurrected, or translated, bodies over those who are still living in natural bodies. The conditions on earth will be glorious. Some see the nations as converted, while others see them as only acquiescing. I am of the view that the nations come to the knowledge of God. Long life and prosperity will be their lot. The period will conclude with one last rebellion. Most futurists are premillennialists. There are also those who support the historical approach and believe in a literal millennium.

The amillennial view holds that the thousand-year reign is symbolic of the present rule of the Church, either by the saints who reign with Yeshua from heaven or the progressive reign of believers on earth. At the end of this Church Age, which is defined as the millennium, Yeshua will return and establish the new heaven and earth. The passages in the Hebrew Bible that predict a long, natural life on this earth are interpreted symbolically. Amillennialists might hold a similar view of the upheavals of the Last Days as premillennialists or they might lean toward a more symbolic or preterist view of the Book of Revelation.

The postmillennialists believe that the Church will so progress in spreading the Gospel that the whole world will come into a glorious age, either a literal or a symbolic thousand years after which there will be a brief rebellion and the Second Coming of Yeshua. The postmillennialists are mostly preterist in interpreting the book of Revelation, so they see no great future tribulation to come, and although there may be some upheavals, the Church will continue to progress.

The Passover: Key to Interpreting Revelation

My approach to the Book of Revelation is not only the product of study, but of a revelation from the Spirit of God. I do not expect you to simply accept this claim. However, if the interpretation put forth here is true to the evidence and powerfully opens the book to you, I encourage you to see this approach as from the Lord.

About two years before the writing of this introduction for the first edition, I believe the Lord spoke to me, "If you want to understand the Book of Revelation, the key is the Passover and Exodus from Egypt." *Spirit-inspired reflection upon this gives me a dramatic sense that the Book of Revelation is most relevant to the generation that lives before the return of Yeshua and that the events of the Revelation parallel the Exodus in amazing ways.*

The people of God in the Last Days are a counterpart to the Jews at the time of the Exodus. The Anti-Messiah and his system parallel pharaoh and the Egyptian system. Some biblical scholars have noted Passover–Exodus similarities in the Book of Revelation. However, I do not know of any who have used Passover–Exodus as a total interpretive key for the Last Days' people of God. I believe the body of the Messiah is involved in events throughout this book, not absent from them and looking down at the tribulation from heaven.

An Overview of Events in Exodus

The Passover–Exodus account describes the people of God as being engaged in a severe struggle with Egypt and her ruler, Pharaoh. For the sake of Israel and of his own purposes in the earth, God raised up two prophets, Moses and Aaron, who announced plagues upon Egypt. The first nine plagues did not result in the repentance of the Egyptians or their leader. The tenth plague, the deaths of the Egyptian firstborns, resulted in Pharaoh releasing the children of Israel. During these plagues, God supernaturally made a distinction between the Egyptians and the children of Israel by protecting the children of Israel in the land of Goshen. Even the most severe plague, the death of the firstborns, did not touch Israel because the Israelites placed the blood of the Passover lamb upon the entry ways to their dwellings.

After the Israelites left, Pharaoh's heart was once again hardened. He pursued the Israelites to the edge of the sea. Israel was hemmed in by water on one side and the soldiers of Egypt on the other. Although they were protected from the forces of Egypt by the pillars of fire and cloud, there appeared to be no way of escape. Then God told Moses to go forward. When he stretched his rod over the sea, the waters parted and the Israelites passed through on dry ground. The amazingly foolish Egyptians pursued Israel into the sea. At God's command, the waters came together and Pharaoh's army was drowned. The astonished people of Israel found themselves on the other side with no one in pursuit. Israel was free; she could now receive the Covenant of God and enter the land of promise.

As you will see in the following chapters, the parallels to this in the Book of Revelation are truly amazing. This truth can have great implications for how the people of God see and pass through the prophesied trials and battles.

With these thoughts in mind, we now turn to the Book of Revelation itself. As I prepared for Passover, 1990, the Lord gave me seven key themes for the Book of Revelation that are connected to Exodus: the preparation of God's People, the plagues of God, God's People protected, the anti-Messiah—the Last Day's Pharaoh, the Exodus rapture, the wrath of the Lamb and his armies, and entry into the eternal Promised Land. Further preparation for this book came through a study of the Book of Isaiah over a six-month period. I believe that the three most important sources for understanding the Book of Revelation are the Hebrew accounts of Passover-Exodus, and Israel's entrance into the Promised Land; the Book of Isaiah; and the Book of Daniel. Most of the themes of the Book of Revelation are anticipated in these writings. We will refer frequently to these materials.

May you be blessed as you read this text along with the Book of Revelation. May you be prepared for spiritual warfare!

CHAPTER ONE

God's Overall Plan for Redemption– A Heavenly View

This chapter gives the view of the unseen battle occurring throughout history and especially throughout the rest of Revelation as discussed in Revelation 12.

Given the unique structure of Revelation, a heavenly prologue to and overview of the Last Days' action is found in the excursus[2] of Revelation 12. Revelation 12 focuses on what events like Jesus' birth and Resurrection look like in the context of the spiritual war being waged between God and Satan. These events set up the climatic battle that follows and give a picture of the sweep of history concerning Israel, the Messiah, and the Church.

As the events describe unfold, it is evident that God uses the earlier occurrences to prepare his People for what is to come—a major theme in both Exodus and Revelation.

---

2. In excursus, there are overlaps. Chronological progression is not carried through from one such passage to another. For example, Revelation 12 includes information from before the birth of Jesus through the Last Days' persecution of Israel and the Church. Parallel visions describe the same events from different perspectives in different parts of the book. The seals, trumpets, and bowls provide the chronological pattern, and the excursus fills in the detail.

The Battle Surrounding a Baby

This excursus begins with a great sign in the heavens. The great sign is a woman, clothed with the sun, standing on the moon, and wearing a garland of twelve stars on her head. The symbolism is rich. To be clothed with the sun is to be wrapped in the light of God. The position of the moon—under the woman's feet—represents dominion. The crown of stars shows her regal standing. The twelve stars correlates to the twelve tribes of Israel. The woman symbolizes Israel, God's Chosen People. She is in labor with a child, according to verse 2.

Verse 3 introduces us to another sign in heaven: a great, fiery red dragon with seven heads crowned with seven diadems and ten horns. The image of the beast parallels the beast with ten horns at the end of Daniel 7. The dragon itself is Satan, the old serpent represented in Isaiah 27 as the leviathan whom God will punish (see Rev. 20:17). The number seven gives a sense of perfect or complete authority; ten also stands as a number of completeness. Those numbers could correspond to the rulership of either progressive emperors or sub-rulers of various Roman provinces. The parallel to the days of the Roman Empire and the Last Days is noteworthy because the dragon's last showcase of power will be similar to its approach in the first century. The dragon, Satan, manifests himself through political leadership of the human realm. Note, too, that Israel's lot throughout history has been the dragon's persecution, both the Nation as a whole and the Messianic Jewish remnant. This history of persecution prepares the Nation for the trying times to come and provides them with a pattern of God's faithfulness that they can cling to when they are targeted.

In verse 4, the action begins as the dragon's tail sweeps a third of the stars to earth, signifying Satan's alliance with a third of the angels in his rebellion. Note that stars can represent angelic leaders, human leaders, or both in scriptural symbolism. Israel, the woman,[3] is ready to give birth, and the dragon waits ready to devour the child, knowing the child is the source of man's redemption. This child is none other than Yeshua the Messiah, who is to rule "all nations with a rod of iron" (Rev. 12:5). Yeshua rules with his Church, so the reference to ruling with a rod of iron is applied to the Church in Revelation 2:26–27. It is clear that Satan is seeking to destroy Yeshua and his work from the time of his birth until his death on the cross. First, Herod was Satan's instrument, commanding the slaughter of the babies around Bethlehem. The religious leaders sought to kill him before his time. Finally, in the Garden of Gethsemane, I believe Satan attempted to kill the

---

3. We have significant variation among scholars. Catholics have traditionally seen the woman as Mary and her corporate union as a symbol of the Church, which includes Old Testament faithful—Israel. Grant Osborn sees the woman as Israel in Revelation 12:17 but sees her representing the Church after the Ascension of Yeshua (see *Revelation*, Grand Rapids, Mich.: Baker, 2006). Yet, Osborn notes here as well that in Glassen and Phillip Hughes the woman represents the Palestinian church, and the gentile church is the offspring (p. 456). Yet how is it that the woman changes her identity after the Ascension? Craig Keener supports the symbol of the woman as Israel, or the faithful remnant of Israel, but that it grows into the symbol of the Church (see *Revelation, The NIV Application Commentary,* [Grand Rapids, Mich.: Zondervan, 2000], p. 314). Remember it is Israel who brings forth the child. This is closer to the truth in my view. In Richard Bauckham, *The Theology of the Book of Revelation,* (Cambridge: Cambridge University Press, 1993), the woman is Eve and Zion from whom the Messiah is born (p. 89). Later he notes that this is the mother of Yeshua. "The symbol is the mother of Yeshua and Christians. She is in symbol Eve, Mary, Israel, Zion, and the church all combined in the image of the covenant people of God" (p. 128). David Stern in the *Jewish New Testament Commentary,* (Clarksville, Md.: Jewish New Testament Publications, 1992), agrees with my understanding that the woman represents Israel, a Jewish woman, and especially Messianic Jews, and the rest of her offspring are the gentile believers (p. 823, 826). This is the most natural way to understand the passage. Stern notes that image is drawn from Isaiah 66:7–10.

Lord.[4]After his Resurrection, Yeshua ascended to the Father or,as it says in verse 5, He was "caught up to God and to his throne." At this point, the text shifts from the Gospel parallels into a symbolic heavenly view of the Revelation's events.

God's Protective Hand

In verse 6 the woman flees into the wilderness to a place of protection prepared by God, one of the key themes found in both Revelation and the Exodus. This wilderness time is described as 1,260 days, or three and half years. Some have taken this to be a literal time period for the worst part of the seven-year tribulation. It is intense but only half of the full measure of suffering during that time.

However, and this will be illustrated later in greater detail, God still places a protective hand on his People as the calamity and destruction fall around them—just as he did when the plagues fell on Egypt but did not impact the Israelites. God's wrath does not fall on the faithful and unbelieving; he does not abandon his children to judgment. He adopts them into his care for safekeeping.

Spiritual Warfare: First in Heaven, Then on Earth

The initial conflict of verse 4 is expanded in verses 7–9. Here the war between the faithful angels of God and the fallen angels

---

4.   This is one of the historical interpretations of the battle of prayer in Gethsemane. In this interpretation, Yeshua prayed that he might be able to succeed and that his suffering would not prematurely issue in his death. The other view is that Yeshua was praying for a way to avoid the cross, or the heavy weight of bearing the sins of the world. Those who hold to the first view believe that Yeshua would not have waivered. In both interpretations, God protected Yeshua.

of Satan is unleashed. The fighting is fierce. Michael, the head of the Lord's army, and his hosts prevail, and Satan's angels are cast out of the heaven to earth (the lower atmosphere). Satan, the one who makes false accusations against the brethren, has been cast down.

The Secret Weapon—The Blood of the Lamb

A voice from heaven calls out, and its promise reveals another level of God's protection for his children—the blood of the Lamb: "And they overcame him by the blood of the Lamb and by the word of their testimony, and they did not love their lives to the death" (v. 11).

A believer's appeal to righteousness through the blood of the Lamb silences the Accuser and unleashes the power of God to resist the Devil and to cause him to flee.[5] Just like the blood of the sacrificial lamb in Exodus protected Israel's firstborn children, the blood of Yeshua, the Lamb of God, protects the body of believers from Satan's anger and retaliation. God pronounces woe upon the earth because it is where Satan seeks to thwart God's plan and destroy mankind. This occurs throughout history but intensifies in the Last Days when Satan's time is very short. This woe is unleashed in the form of plagues that attack the earth and its inhabitants—just as God sent plagues to punish Egypt for their hard-heartedness.

The blood of the Lamb also illustrates how God prepares his People. Sending Yeshua as the Messiah was part of God's ultimate plan for redeeming mankind and preparation for bringing back his Chosen People. The power of the blood that

---

5. Bauckham interestingly sees the blood of the Lamb in Revelation 12:11 as referring to the blood of the martyrs by which they have overcome the tribulation (p. 76). Their blood belongs to the Lamb.

allows believers to overcome also was part of God's plan all along. He prepared his People for the Great Tribulation and set up everything in advance of the Last Days.

The Battle on Earth

The dragon, thrown down from heaven, persecutes the woman (v. 13) on earth. The winged beast, representing Satan, doggedly pursues to kill the woman, symbolizing corporate Israel and the Messianic Jewish community.[6]God gives the woman the wings of an eagle so she can fly away to safety. The wings of eagles is a symbol from Exodus 19:47 where Israel escapes from Egypt. She is ultimately protected in the wilderness for "Times, time, and half a time" (v. 14), and survives the attacks of the Devil. The time frame mentioned in verse 14 is often seen as the aforementioned three and a half years (v. 6). The woman is protected from the floods of water that are poured out against her. This does not mean that Israel will not suffer awesome persecution and destruction, but in the ultimate sense, just as the Israelites in Goshen were protected from the plagues against Egypt, Israel will be protected and survive the plagues of the tribulation.

The dragon, enraged that he cannot overcome the woman (Israel)"went to make war with the rest of her offspring, who keep the commandments of God and have the testimony of Jesus Christ" (v. 17). Persecution is expanded to include Gentiles. The Church is the offspring of Israel and a Jewish-rooted People. Together, Israel and the Church represent two parts of God's unified plan for world redemption (Rom. 11).

---

6. Keener sees an Exodus parallel here in that Satan pursues the woman just as Pharaoh pursued Israel into the desert (p. 322).

Therefore, the same Devil, who seeks to destroy Israel, seeks to destroy the Church. This has been true throughout history but will be especially so at the end of this transitional age.

As God ultimately protects Israel, so he protects his faithful remnant of Messianic Jews and their brothers and sisters from all nations through his supernatural power at work in them and by the blood of the Lamb. There will be cities of refuge and areas where God's People are in control. There is ultimate protection even for those called to martyrdom. Not a hair of their heads will be lost (Luke 21:18). Indeed, his faithful people will ultimately rule and reign with him in complete victory— and on to the eternal Promised Land.

From here the text plunges into the earthly happenings of the End Times, as influenced by the unseen war raging in the heavens. The spiritual warfare of the Last Days and its effect on the human domain are detailed and violent. But as indicated here, God has always protected his Chosen People—and he will continue to do so even in the End Times.

CHAPTER TWO

Preparation of God's People

The theme of the preparation of
God's People is found in Revelation 1–4.

With the knowledge of the Revelation 12 excursus, we turn to the beginning of Revelation, where the aged apostle, John, describes how he was given his vision of the Last Days. These first four chapters all reiterate a main theme of both Revelation and Exodus—God prepares his People for the events to come.

John's Description of the Setting of his Revelation

John was exiled on the island of Patmos. The visions and words of Revelation came to him in an extraordinary rapture in the Holy Spirit. The natural mind cannot understand this. Scholars who understand the Book of Revelation merely as a composition using the literary devices and symbols common to the author's day completely miss the point. Of course, the revelation given to John was presented in terms that could be understood by the first-century reader, but it also was given in terms that will be best understood by the People of God in the Last Days! However, John's testimony must be taken at face value.

He was in the Spirit and had an experience with the Lord in which he was given this prophecy. God gave symbols and words that would speak to the understanding of his contemporaries. Revelation 1:3 reads, "Blessed is he who reads and those who hear the words of this prophecy, and keep those things which are written in it; for the time is near." These words harken to the foreshadowing of Joel 2:28–32, indicating that God's People have been living in the Last Days since the outpouring of the Holy Spirit. The finale of these Last Days will take place for the last generation of this transitional age, just prior to the return of Yeshua the Messiah. However, it is God's intention that every generation be able to see themselves and their struggles in the terms of Revelation.

The first-century believers had a vivid sense that they could be the age's last generation. Many had lived through events like the ones typified in Revelation: the persecution and scattering of Israel, the persecution of the saints, and the fall of "Babylon" and its religious system (the fall of Rome). Yet the events of the early centuries that fulfill and parallel the prophecy in Revelation in no way detract from the fact that the fullest manifestations of its meaning will be for the generation of the Second Coming.[7] Believers encountering severe spiritual warfare are to see themselves as perhaps the last generation before the return of the Lord. In prophetic time and application, "the time is near."

Similar to the situation of the early Church was Israel in Exodus. They had been enslaved by Egypt and ruled cruelly. The Israelites had no leadership and continued to cry of to their God for redemption. God heard their cries and responded, sending Moses and Aaron to encourage their faith and persevere.

---

7.   Osborn argues that the preterist element does not detract from the final battles and futurist dimension of the book (p. 1). Keener also notes that the book applies not only to the time it was written, but also to all times (p. 154). Both of these conclusions reinforce my view expressed in the Introduction of this book.

The Seven Churches of Asia Minor

After explaining how he came to have this vision, John turns to address the seven churches of Asia Minor and sends them messages of encouragement. He proclaims the victory of Yeshua the Messiah and the body's co-rule with him as kings and priests to God. All of the tribes of the earth will mourn, and the nations will at last turn to the Lord at his coming (Zech. 14, Isa. 45:22–25).[8]

The seven churches of Asia Minor (modern Turkey) were churches for which John was responsible as an apostle, according to early Church fathers such as Papias. John is writing to real churches that are undergoing or will soon undergo a real trial.

Note the importance of this. Many interpreters, following the example of nineteenth-century dispensationalists, have too easily identified the seven churches as seven progressive periods of Church history. Nineteenth-century dispensationalists viewed themselves as the Philadelphian church, the only commended group in John's letters. They taught that the Laodicean Age was beginning, and they saw themselves in an overlapping period. Hence, they viewed the concept of being kept from the hour of trial as a promise that the true Church would ascend to heaven before the seven-year tribulation began and the Bride of the Messiah would be absent from the Great Tribulation. I believe this dispensational teaching is wrong and

---

8. The mourning of all tribes of the earth is interpreted negatively and positively as real repentance. Stern takes it to mean the Land of Israel and her repentance and as parallel to Zechariah 12:10. Perhaps worldwide mourning in most commentators is parallel to mourning in Israel. I take this to mean world repentance and to be understood positively in the light of the prophetic promise of the conversion of the nations at the end (Isa. 2, 11)

impractical. The promise for the Philadelphians is meant for all true believers for the trials, plagues, and other judgments that follow in Revelation. However, this does not mean the Church will rapture before the Great Tribulation.

First, as discussed more fully in the next chapter, God can protect his People without removing them from the earth entirely, keeping them from the hour of trial. This also does not mean that some will not be called to sanctify the Name of God as martyrs. Even though some will die, Jesus promised that not a hair on a believer's head would be lost (Luke 21:18). This is how complete the promise of the Resurrection is. Some are kept from the trial by being able to sing through the flames as Ridley and Latimer did in seventeenth-century England; others will be kept in supernatural protection in refuges like Goshen in Exodus. No matter what God's manner of safekeeping, believers will not be subject to his judgment and will only be accountable to the Spirit of God concerning their witness in the Last Days.[9]

Second, those who believe in the restoration of the body of believers to unity, power, love, holiness, and glory before Jesus comes see a problem with the Laodiceans representing the Church's state just before the rapture. This view does not take into account the importance of spiritual warfare in the development of those qualities. It is true that one of these churches might be more characteristic of a given period in

---

9.   Stern argues that Revelation 3:10 is parallel to the promise of Revelation 7—when God seals and protects his People during the world trial—and he adds that this corresponds with the rest of the book (p. 800). Hence, Revelation 3:10 anticipates one of my primary seven thematic concepts for interpretation, God's People protected, anticipating also that the sealing is more than just for Messianic Jews. Protection is a constant theme according to Bauckham. He notes many times that protection does not entail that one might not be called to martyrdom (p. 78, 79).

Church history or of a church within a particular geographic location. For example, some have said the late twentieth-century American church is Laodicean but certainly that statement would not apply to the Church in the Third World or China during that same time! Indeed, many of the problems associated with the seven churches are found in churches of every age. Although there may be great applications for churches today and great warnings for the Church in the Last Days, I believe that the intended messages of these texts are for the seven first-century Asia Minor churches, which is the view of all non-dispensational interpreters including the ones referenced in this book.

In Revelation 1:12–13 John has a great vision of Yeshua, "One like the Son of Man," in the midst of seven lampstands. The seven lampstands are the light of the Holy Spirit's power and testimony shining forth from the seven churches. Seven is the number of perfection. As seen in other texts (such as in Zechariah), the Holy Spirit is the oil that gives the ability to lamps to burn. Yeshua is the testimony of the churches; he is in the midst of the lampstands. Verse 20 makes the interpretation of the symbols clear:

> "The mystery of the seven stars which you saw in my right hand, and the seven golden lampstands: The seven stars are the angels of the seven churches, and the seven lampstands which you saw are the seven churches."

Some have interpreted the "seven angels" to be the head pastors of each church because the word *angel* can also mean, "messenger." (This is the basis of the Baptist tradition of calling pastoral delegates to governing conventions "messengers.") Because John writes to the angel of each church, it is probable that he is not speaking of a church's guardian angel but of a human leader who can receive the word. It is possible that these churches were of such a size that the leaders were not local pastors in modern terms, but overseers of several congregations.

The Letters to the Seven Churches

The seven letters precede the prophecies because the Church must be zealous and holy to face the spiritual warfare of the Last Days. Only then will victory be assured. Those who are not holy and full of God will succumb to the enemy. Therefore, these letters are a preparation for God's People. Even though these letters were addressed to these specific first-century churches, they all have tremendous implications for God's People in the Last Days. If the body of the Messiah can overcome[10] the warnings of these letters and be restored, the Church will become the glorious Bride, without spot or wrinkle, and will enter into the victory of the Lord.

The Church of Ephesus

The first church addressed in Revelation 2:1–7 is the church of Ephesus. Although commended for testing apostles, showing patience and perseverance, and laboring for the Lord, the

---

10. All of the promises outlined in the following letters to the churches are for all who overcome—*all* believers of *all* ages. Those who overcome will not be hurt by the second death as described in Revelation 20 as a final separation from God. John does not contemplate salvation for people who only give lip service to the Kingdom of God!

church is severely warned for having left her first love. She is called to repent to not lose her lampstand (the power of witness through the Spirit). The Church is also commended for rejecting the Nicolaitans, which some scholars believe combined Gnostic heresies with their biblical faith. (Gnostics were heretics who taught that secret knowledge and mysteries were the means of salvation.)

From this letter believers can learn the primary faith challenge of the believer and the corporate body is to maintain a fervent love for the Lord. All acceptable works flow from this love, which is crucial preparation for the battle to come and every trial in life. This alone enables the maintaining of righteous motives. Meditating on what the Lord has done and promised stirs this love. A constant infusion of the Holy Spirit (Eph. 5:18) also maintains this love. God commanded the sons of Israel to love him with all their heart, soul, and strength (Deut. 6:5); the New Covenant promises the ability to fulfill the command. Radical love for God and his Son is the key preparation for the Last Days. The reward for overcoming is eating from the tree of life in God's paradise.

The Church of Smyrna

Revelation 2:8–11 describes the church of Smyrna that has been persecuted. Some of this came from Jewish impostors (those not born Jewish but who took on Jewish practices and persecuted the believers who did not—or those from the Jewish leadership who pressured the believers with false doctrine, accusations, and attempts to woo believers away from the truth). Her tribulation will last ten days (a number that symbolizes completion).

The call is for all believers to be fearless. Fearlessness is a product of fervent love and faith in God, which is fully present even during a severe trial. This is a major step of preparation for all believers in the End Times. Such faith is built through a life that includes the discipline of meditating on the Lord's promises and seeing them established in a believer's life as reflections of God's character. The reward for faithfulness even unto death is the crown of life (resurrection and co-rule with Messiah).

The Church of Pergamos

In Revelation 2:12–17 the Pergamos church has also experienced persecution. Satan has a throne in Pergamos, which could indicate the empire's false religious system or other false cults. The Pergamos believers did not deny Jesus even when they lost a faithful martyr,[11] Antipas.

Despite these reasons for commendation, the church at Pergamos is rebuked for holding to the teaching of Balaam, who sought money for his prophetic ability. He also led Israel to commit sexual immorality so that she would lose her favor with God and the pagan King Balak could defeat her. John also mentions the Nicolaitans here. Did these Nicolaitans teach a sexual liberty (like the later libertarian Gnostics) as part of grace? If this were so, they would, thus, be tools of Satan to spiritually weaken believers so that he could defeat the church. The church is called to repent or be subject to the Lord's severe judgment.

Godly congregations must discipline those who violate of basic biblical doctrine and morality. Those who overcome are

---

11. The word *martyr* means "witness." The early Church understood that the highest witness was testimony given in the face of death.

promised hidden manna (the treasures of the Word of God) and a white stone with a new name. The latter typifies a gem reflecting a true believer's new name, which refers to his/her distinctive character and calling in the Kingdom of God.

The Church of Thyatira

The church at Thyatira is also commended for faith, patience, and works (v. 19). However, a woman named Jezebel is tolerated. She is a false prophetess who beguiles the servants of God to commit sexual immorality and eat food sacrificed to idols. She was given time to repent, but now severe judgment is decreed upon her and upon those who commit adultery with her.

Apparently Jezebel beguiled the church into secret doctrines called "the depths of Satan" (v. 24). Again, this has Gnostic overtones. Some have noted that the characteristics of Jezebel in this chapter are amazingly similar to those of King Ahab's Queen Jezebel. (This has led to a teaching in the Charismatic church concerning a principality of Jezebel, an evil power that causes destructive, manipulative patterns in the Church when yielded to.) Perhaps even in this section of Revelation, Jezebel is not the actual name of the woman but is used because there are parallels to the same sins of Israel's former queen.

A Jezebelian work is characterized by manipulative prophecy—the broadcasting of strange doctrine and the domination of weak men for Satan's advantage, especially when there is no strong governing male eldership. Amazingly, this condition produces spiritual impotence in the men and a diminishing of the Spirit's real gifts among the people. As Queen Jezebel demoralized Elijah, so men sometimes feel powerless. This situation sometimes leads to actual sexual immorality. (I have seen this problem many times in various churches throughout my last twenty years of ministry.)

The Thyatirans are promised a part in ruling the nations if they overcome. The fact that Psalm 2:8–9 is quoted is significant. The psalm promises the Messiah's rule over the nations with a rod of iron. This strong rule is here applied to the Bride of the Messiah. His rule is a co-rule with believers. Therefore, the psalm is interpreted as applying to all who overcome.

The call is to hold fast to God's teachings and do not allow any attack to loosen the grip on what is true and righteous. The gift of the morning star means participation in the revelation of his coming, which signals the full transformation of believers as sons of God (Rom. 8:19). Indeed, his appearance leads to the dawn of the millennium.

The Church of Sardis

Revelation 3:1–6 focuses on the Sardis church. This group has significant activity but is primarily dead works. Because only works that proceed from a heart of love for the Lord are perfect, the believers at Sardis are called to repent. The warnings are severe, even to the point of calling into question the salvation. The Lord will come as a thief to those who perform mere good works of the flesh but do not truly know and walk with him. These works are defiling. First Thessalonians 5 makes it clear that those who are not in darkness will find that the Lord's coming does not overtake them like a thief. The seven spirits mentioned in the text are usually noted as the perfection of the Spirit in the symbol of seven, and the seven stars are again the perfection of angelic powers of those who serve God.

All believers must love God with a pure heart—only then can their works be seen as alive in God's eyes. The promise for those who are worthy is to wear the white garments of purity and priesthood and have their names inscribed in the Book of Life.

The Church of Philadelphia

The Philadelphian church is discussed in Revelation 3:7–13. This congregation is praised above all. The Messiah, Yeshua, has the key of David and is in control of opening and closing opportunities for his People. This church is also under persecution from the synagogue of Satan (either false converts to Judaism or groups of Jews who were perverting gospel teaching). Those of that "synagogue" will bow before the Philadelphians. These believers will be kept from the hour of trial, which will come upon all the earth.

God honors those who prove faithful in the face of persecution and attack. Those who overcome will be pillars in God's Temple, marked by the Name of God, and part of the everlasting New Jerusalem (Rev. 21:9–21). They will be given new names, showing forth their eternal callings and nature in the Messiah.

The Church of Laodicea

Revelation 3:13–22 describes the lukewarm Laodicean church. God hates a lukewarm nature and will spit them out. Blinded to their true condition, the Laodiceans see themselves as spiritually strong and wealthy. This wealth need not necessarily include great material riches but could include financial means. Yet God proclaims the true condition of this church, "Wretched, miserable, poor, blind and naked" (v. 17). The healing of this condition requires the purchase of gold refined in the fire; white garments for clothing; and salve to restore sight. This includes the act of repentance, covering sin by the blood of the Lamb and rekindling of the fire of love for the Father, the Lord Jesus, and the Holy Spirit. Only when this love burns within can cleansing occur. Only then can spiritual perception be solidified. John reminds the church that God rebukes those he loves. He chastens only his children (Heb. 12:5–11). He waits for man to approach him and accept the great invitation to a feast of fellowship (v. 20).

A believer must offer God his whole life and keeping nothing back. It is noteworthy that those who overcome are promised a place with the Lord on his throne. (See also Ephesians 2:6 for a description of a Spirit-filled believer's life as seated with God in heaven. This promise completes the picture of Ephesians and parallels Revelation 2:26–27.)

John Is Called to Heaven

Revelation 4 begins with John being called to heaven,[12] lifting the veil between heaven and earth. John sees into the unseen world, which has such a great effect on the seen world (and vice versa). John is called to heaven and told that he will see things that will come to pass—it is a vision of what God is preparing his People for. When God grants such an experience, the person is not conscious of his physical being. (Paul stated

---

12. Some have also seen this as a reference to the rapture of the saints before the Great Tribulation. This is improbable because John is called up to see the rest of the vision and it is not a prophecy of a future event.

that he knew a man who was called up to heaven. The man did not know whether that man was in his body [2 Cor. 12:2–4]. Most commentators believe that Paul is speaking of himself and uses this language as a form of humility.) In such experiences location and physicality are transcended.

From here on, the visions of the rest of the Revelation certainly take on a literal slant for those familiar with the symbolism of the Hebrew Scriptures and the book's first-century setting. However, it is difficult to distinguish figurative from literal meaning because John is telling us what he saw, but these realities might or might not forever appear in heaven. Is this God-authored description the best understanding of realities that go beyond what can be literally put forth? Are there really creatures that look like the ones described as full of eyes (v. 6), or is this a symbol of a spiritual reality? It is undeterminable from the text itself.

In the opening verses of Revelation 4, John sees God as jasper and sardius stone in appearance. An emerald rainbow hangs over the throne, which is surrounded by twenty-four thrones. Twenty-four elders clothed in white robes with crowns of gold on their heads sit on these thrones. The possibilities for interpretation of these twenty-four elders[13] are many and not necessarily exclusive. The number twenty-four is a multiple of twelve. There are twelve tribes of Israel and twelve original apostles, corresponding to the names on the gates and the foundation stones of the New Jerusalem (Rev. 21). Are these twenty-four the corporate representation of the Old and New

---

13. See G. R. Beasley–Murray, *The Revelation: New Bible Commentary,* (Grand Rapids, Mich.: Eerdmans, 1970). He expresses the twenty-four elders as symbolic of the People of God in both pre- and post-Yeshua times. Note as well that these elders bow down before Yeshua and worship him, a very strong testimony to his deity.

Testament saints before God's throne? Is it possible that the elders are the actual presence of the twelve patriarchs and twelve apostles before the throne? Both of these are possibilities. The twenty-four corporately represent the continual praise of all God's People before the throne of grace. This also does not exclude the spiritual presence of each individual believer as seated with Christ in heavenly places (Eph. 2:6). The white robes are the garb of priestly service and purity. The crowns represent the reward of eternal fruit and the authority of rule. Both of which are promised to those who overcome.

The descriptions of the sea of glass, the lamps burning, and the four living creatures are a picture of awesome majesty. The seven lamps represent the perfection (in the number seven) of the presence of the Spirit (in the lamps). The qualities of the living creatures around the throne represent the majesty and rule of the lion, the intelligence and quality of man in the image of God, the swiftness of the eagle, and the steadiness of the calf. The many eyes represent a fullness of vision. Four could indicate universality in rule, corresponding to the number of compass points—north, south, east, and west. The picture of continual rapturous worship is beyond comprehension. The living creatures cry out, "Holy, holy, holy," and the twenty-four elders fall down before him, casting their crowns in submission, because their ruler is fully under the Father. The hymn of praise is glorious:"You are worthy, O Lord, to receive glory and honor and power; for you created all things, and by your will they exist and were created" (v. 11).

Revelation 5 states that the figure represented upon the throne is none other than the Father because the Son will take a scroll from him. This is reminiscent of the picture of the Son receiving rule from the Ancient of Days in Daniel 7. The Lamb's acceptance of the scroll begins the passages concerning God's judgment.

This passage parallels Exodus as well. The burning bush is the first revelation in the symbol of fire. This encounter with God is where God gives Moses his plan for Israel's redemption from slavery. He shares with Moses his directives on how to be prepared to face Pharaoh and how to prepare God's People for what is to come. He assures Moses of victory and his awesome identity.[14]

---

14.   The quality of supernatural vision also intensifies later when Moses climbs the mountain with the elders of Israel. The pavement of sapphire stone is described as having the clarity of the heavens. The amazing account describes eating and drinking in the presence of God. This also parallels John's vision of the heavenly realm.

CHAPTER THREE

The Plagues of God
on Worldwide Egypt

*This chapter covers the themes of God's People protected
and the plagues as described in Revelation 5–9.*

With the completion of God's preparation of his People
through John's messages, judgment can now begin in the form
of various plagues that wreak havoc. But before God unleashes
his wrath upon the earth, he first turns to protect the body of
believers. Just like God protected the Israelites when the plagues
struck Egypt, he will isolate those who believe in him from
the forthcoming harm. In Revelation these two themes—the
plagues and protection—are woven together, as the devastation
intensifies, and directly parallel the action in Exodus. God's
protection begins before the tribulation ensues and continues as
the plagues destroy the people and land on earth.

The Sealing of the 144,000 (Rev. 7:1–8)

Before moving into the judgment phase of Revelation, it is
necessary to interrupt the order of the text with an excursus from
Revelation 7. Here there are four angels at the four corners of
the earth who contain the four winds, keeping these gales from
blowing. These winds, once released, increase heat and suffering.
Another angel appears, holding the seal of the living God. He

ascends from the east to command the four angels who have the power to harm the earth and the sea. His command is that they do nothing until the servants of God have seals placed upon their foreheads. The plagues are God's judgment on those who have not turned to him and whose hearts are hard, like Pharaoh in Exodus, and that judgment will not fall upon committed believers. *Just as Israel was protected in the land of Goshen in Exodus 8:22, so God's servants throughout the world will be sealed and protected.[15]I believe the prophetic words coming forth today concerning cities of refuge in the Last Days is true. Not only will there be protection of individuals, but also God will lead his People to places of refuge, like Goshen was in Egypt. It is my belief that believers in these places will also protect the Jewish people. One commentator, S. MacLean Gilmore, connects the seals on believers' foreheads with the protection granted Israelite households during Passover.[16] Israelite families outlined the doorposts of their homes with the blood of a lamb, and the angel of death did not touch their firstborn children. Faith in the blood of the Lamb—Yeshua—offers the same safeguarding here.*

Who Is Sealed?

Verse 4 speaks of who is sealed: "And I heard the number of those who were sealed. One hundred and forty-four thousand of all the tribes of the children of Israel were sealed..."

Varying interpretations have been applied to verse 4 as scholars try to define who exactly is noted in the "all of the

15. The sense of protection for faithful believers was also seen in Chapter 1's discussion of Revelation 12, where protection is offered through the blood of the Lamb, and will be discussed further in Chapters 5's description of the rapture.

16. See Gilmore, "The Revelation of St. John," in *The Interpreter's One Volume Commentary on the Bible*, (New York: Abington, 1971), p. 955.

tribes of the children of Israel." Does this mean that only people of Jewish or Israelite descent are sealed? How do believers from all nations fit in? There is a wide range in interpretation. Some have taught that this must mean that the Church is no longer on the earth during the tribulation because the only remaining representative of the People of God is Israel! This seems unlikely because it would mean that Revelation, which was written for believers to read (Rev. 22:6, 9–10), would not apply directly to any in the Bride of the Messiah!

Another conclusion is that the 144,000 sealed represent the Church. While sealing is presented only for the 144,000, there are many reasons to think that this sealing is for more than just the Jewish believers. David Stern connects the promise made to the Church of Philadelphia of being kept from the hour of trial (Rev. 3:10) to the sealing of the 144,000.[17] Some point to verses 5–8, which say 12,000 are from each tribe listed, noting that the tribe of Dan is absent from this roll.[18] These scholars also note that today the tribes are indistinguishable. Therefore, some say the twelve tribes are symbolic of the body of believers as a whole and this passage refers to spiritual Israel, not natural Israel.[19]

---

17.   Stern, p. 810.

18.   Was this because Dan first led Israel toward idolatry, as recorded in the Book of Judges?

19.   Osborn asserts that these are symbolic of the Church (p. 311, 312). Keener seeing the 144,000 as the saved Jewish remnant is credible (p. 231). His reasons are the woman connected to Israel in Revelation 12 (see Chapter 1), and a massive evidence of a great End Time turning to faith among the Jewish People. Yet later, he goes on to argue that this group also is portraying all believers. The larger group of scholars, which follows a less literal presentation of the 144,000, believes that the multitude is from all nations. Bauckham argues that the sealed 144,000 contrast the multitude from every nation (mentioned later in this section), but "the two images constitute the same reality" (p. 76), and therefore both groups represent all nations. It is strange if there is a contrast to identify the two groups.

I do not agree with this view. First of all, I do not believe that the Bible ever uses the words *Israel* or *Jew* as terms for all believers. The scriptural term for believers who are not of Jewish birth is "spiritual seed [children] of Abraham" (Gal. 3:29).[20] Therefore, the only conclusion can be that the 144,000 are Messianic Jews.[21]

Is the Number 144,000 Literal?

The number 144,00 is clearly symbolic: 12 x 12 x 10 x 10 x 10 = 144,000. Twelve is the number of the tribes of Israel and the number of apostles. Ten represents completeness and is multiplied three times, with three representing God. This is the number of the saved remnant of Israel in the Last Days. It may refer only to the saved remnant in the Land, to just the men of this saved remnant, or to the saved of world Jewry. There is a little room for interpretation here.

Personally, I believe the 144,000 is not literal. I believe the number of Messianic Jews during this period will be larger than 144,000 mentioned and will make up between a tenth and a fifth of all Jewish people. In my estimation, this

---

20. Galatians 6:16 and Romans 2 are used to support the spiritual Israel terminology, but I believe this is incorrect, and that this terminology is confusing. Both passages, I believe, refer to Jews or Israelites who are born again and following the pattern of apostolic teaching. I believe that this is the case in Revelation as well.

21. Bauckham argues that the 144,000 are sealed for martyrdom and, therefore, deliverance from the evil world, paralleling to a degree the Exodus the Israelites made through the Red Sea to escape Pharaoh in Exodus 14. "They triumph in heaven while enemies on earth are doomed to final judgment" (p. 79). I find this strange. It is not that I do not accept protection and martyrdom together, but to see both the 144,000 and the great multitude that follows as all martyrs seems a stretch. Here in Revelation, the seal of God prevents harm from the plagues. There is no specific word that this protection is only by martyrdom.

would make the number of redeemed Jews between 1.2 and 3 million. Because the text speaks only of men, if women and children are added, it will be a much larger number. The 144,000 could be close to a literal number of the believing Jewish men in the Land of Israel. Remember in Exodus the Israelites in the Sinai Desert were counted in such a way. With women and children, their number was well more than the 600,000 recorded. Regardless of interpretation, the passage is prophetic concerning a great company of witnesses who are Jewish in the Land of Israel; this is the saved remnant of Israel![22]

What Is the Significance of the Saved Remnant?

Remember Paul was concerned about seeing a remnant of Israel saved as a prelude to her full acceptance of the Lord (Rom. 11:14–15). The saved remnant of Israel is both part of national Israel (or Jews throughout the world), and is the Jewish membership of the body of the Messiah. Will God actually see that 12,000 are saved from each tribe? This is possible. Only he knows descent from the specific tribes of Israel. Some things seen as being symbolic may happen with far more literal fulfillment. However, *although the sealing is specifically applied to the saved remnant of Israel here, I believe the principle of sealing is universal among believers.*

---

22. Stern argues that the 144,000 is a delimited number and, though symbolic, is contrasted with the other group (p. 810). He takes the same position as I do that the 144,000 is the idealization of the Messianic Jews. I do not disagree that Bauckham's position that the 144,000 could include men as well as women. Bauckham views the 144,000 are an army to defeat the gentile oppressors (p. 78). The seal is symbolic of ritual purity, not sexual asceticism, as required by the state for men going off to war (see Revelation 14). The symbol can encompass married and single, male and female. My interpretation above of only men is an assumption as is his assertion. Both conclusions are credible.

This is the implication later in Revelation 9:4, where the locusts are commanded "not to harm the grass of the earth, or any green thing, or any tree, but only those men who do not have the seal of God on their foreheads."[23] There is no distinction in this later text of those being sealed coming only from the tribes of Israel.

The Great Multitude of Saints (Rev. 7:9–17)

The saints from all nations are clearly distinguished from the 144,000. Just as the first part of Revelation 7 spoke of Israel, the second part focuses on the universal people of God from all nations. Evidence for this interpretation is found in that the second group is described in quite different terms:[24]

> ... A great multitude which no one could number,
> of all nations, tribes, peoples, and tongues,
> standing before the throne and before the Lamb,
> clothed with white robes, with palm branches in
> their hands... (Rev. 7:9)

---

23. In *Breaking the Code, Understanding the Book of Revelation.* (Nashville: Abington Press, 1993), Bruce M. Metzger says, "Just as the Israelites had been exempt from the plagues of Egypt, so now the Christians who have God's seal upon their foreheads will be completely unharmed by these awful creatures of divine judgment (9:4)" (p. 65).

24. Metzger sees the first group as a symbol of completeness (p. 60, 61). He notes the contrasts and then says, "In the first vision the throng can be counted; in the second (in Rev. 7:9–17), it is incalculably numerous. In the first it is drawn form the twelve tribes of Israel; in the second, from every nation. In the first, it is being prepared for imminent peril; in the second, it is victorious and secure." This would naturally lead to the conclusion that there are two groups, but then Metzger goes on to say, "The two visions are correlative and refer to the same people distinguished only by their location... the purpose of the second vision is to bring encouragement to believers by revealing what awaits them in heaven."

The members of the multitude cry out in worship, extolling God the Father and the Lamb. As they worship, the four living creatures and the twenty-four elders, mentioned in Revelation 4, fall down and worship as well. Again, the white robes of the multitude are symbols of purity and of priestly ministry. The worship of the saints is joined by the worship of those in heaven. What an extraordinary picture! The saints are in worship and are caught up to the throne. The experience of this reality depends on the quality of unity in worship. The angels and elders join in worship, singing, "Thanksgiving and honor and power and might be to our God forever and ever"(v. 12b).

This picture is a vision of the body of the Messiah, which is described in Ephesians as "seated with him in heavenly places." Through the presence of the Holy Spirit, the believers individually and corporately transcend space and are fully present before the throne of God. Although this is not a reality presently seen by the physical eye, it is a spiritual reality, nonetheless.

One of the elders asks John the identity of this group, and John turns the question back on his interrogator. John is told that this great multitude represents those who have come out of the Great Tribulation—although the members of this group are not specifically described as martyrs or as people who have died[25]—and washed their robes white in the blood of the Lamb. This is a picture of the Last Days' Church of God. The time span covers all the saints who will live through this period. This is a great picture of the unity and purity in

---

25. That this might not be an image primarily of martyrs is also supported by Osborn who sees the position of the saints in Revelation 7 as parallel to the description of Ephesians 2, seated with him in heavenly places. This is seen as a culmination of the priesthood of believers.

the Last Days, for which Yeshua prayed (John 17:20–26) and which Paul predicted would come about (Eph. 4:11–16). This multitude serves God before the throne day and night. This is a worshiping, intercessory people. The Lamb dwells among them, and they are protected from the plagues that embroil the world around them. Again, it is not only the Jewish remnant that is protected, but all true believers are delivered from the hunger, thirst, scorching sun, and beasts that attack the earth. Their destiny is to experience great comfort because God will wipe away all their tears. This is part of God's plan of protection for his People.

Final Judgment—Exodus' Plagues on a Worldwide Scale (Rev. 5–6)

Now that the discussion of God's protection of his People is complete, the focus can turn to the need for protection as described in Revelation 5–6 and 8–9. John describes the scene before the throne of God as everyone waits for the seals on the scroll to be broken.

The Lamb Who Is Worthy Takes the Scroll (Rev. 5:1–14)

Revelation 5 is one of the great inspirational chapters of the Bible. Its symbolism elicits a tremendous sense of holy wonder and awe. In verse 1 the Father holds a scroll in his hand. The scroll is sealed with seven seals. The scroll represents God's decrees concerning the acts of judgment and redemption during the Last Days. The seven seals represent the seven judgments. (Ancient scrolls were sealed in a manner similar to sealing letters, with sealing wax stamping them with the sender's symbol.) No one is found to open this scroll, and John weeps.

Then John is told that the Lion of Judah, Yeshua the Messiah, has prevailed to open the scroll. Here John sees the vision of the Lamb who was slain taking the scroll from the Father's hand (vs. 6–7). The symbolic nature of John's vision becomes clear: Yeshua the Messiah is human and divine—not literally a lamb, nor did he take on the form of a lamb—and so dwells among his People. However, in symbol, the role of Jesus as the sacrificial Lamb is evident. By his sacrifice and Resurrection he has the right to take the scroll and open the seals. I believe that the seals opened by the Lamb give him the authority to initiate all of the judgments that follow.

In verse 8, the four living creatures and the twenty-four elders fall down and worship the Lamb. The divinity of Jesus, who is worthy to receive this level of worship, is well illustrated in the vivid imagery of this verse. The twenty-four elders represent the People of God. They hold golden bowls of incense representing all of the saints' prayers. The harps could represent the worship of the saints. This representative role is illustrated in their singing to the Lamb.[26] Every tribe, tongue, and nation has been redeemed and made kings and priests to God (Rev. 7:14–15), who will reign on earth. Ten thousand times ten thousand angels, as well as many others, join in worship. After this, John hears all of the creatures in the universe join in prayer.

The Seven Seals (Rev. 6:1–17, 8:1–6)

With the seals come the first plagues with parallels in the Exodus story. (Note not all of the plagues of Revelation are represented in the Exodus story; some are unique.) Throughout the rest of

---

26. The reader would do well to meditate on the great hymns found in this chapter.

Revelation, the events on earth are not to be understood in terms of natural causation because there are supernatural dimensions to these earthly events. This integral connection of the seen to the unseen world is far more extensive than realized.

Remember there were ten plagues upon Egypt, with the number ten representing complete judgment. There are twenty-one segments of judgment revealed in the Book of Revelation, including seven seals, seven trumpets, and seven bowls of God's wrath.[27] Twenty-one is the product of three and seven; seven is the number of perfection and three is the number of God; therefore, twenty-one represents God's perfection in judgment. This is perfect and final judgment of the whole world for all time. The seals are progressive. The seventh seal includes the judgments of the seven trumpets, and the seventh trumpet includes the judgments of the seven bowls of God's wrath.[28]Several plagues are similar in type to the plagues upon Egypt. *However, every plague in Revelation is now intensified,*

---

27.   Metzger says on the progression of judgments and the Passover–Exodus connection: "John's description of the series of God's judgments corresponds in some measure to that of the ten plagues sent against the Egyptians in order to persuade pharaoh to let the people of Israel go (Ex. 7–10). The treatment of Christians by Rome can be compared to the enslavement to the Israelites in Egypt and God's judgment on the enemies of the church will be like the plagues on the land and people of ancient Egypt." Bauckham writes, "Since the Exodus was the key salvation event of the history of Israel, in which God liberated his people from oppression in Egypt, destroyed their oppressors, made them his own people and led them to theocratic independence in a land of their own, it was naturally the model for prophetic and apocalyptic hopes of another great salvation event in the future" (p. 70).

28.   Bauckham again provides confirmation of this interpretation: "In other words, the seventh of each series portrays the final act of judgment in which evil is destroyed and God's kingdom arrives. But the three series are so connected that the seventh seal opening includes the seven trumpets and the seventh trumpet includes the seven bowls. Thus each series reaches the same end, but from starting points progressively closer to the end. This is why the three series of judgments are of progressive severity" (p. 40).

both in scope and in the devastating results.[29]*And just as Pharaoh and the Egyptians hardened their hearts despite the plagues, so most of the peoples of the world will harden their hearts toward God.*

The first seal reveals a white horse and a rider with a bow and a crown. He is given the right to conquer. War is loosed upon the earth; this domination produces an increase of power for the conqueror, which could indicate the conquering of world government. Though Pharaoh did not attain to the power and extent of the Roman emperor or the power of the Last Day's anti-Messiah, he does foreshadow both periods as a dominating international leader who oppresses Israel.

The second seal reveals a horseman on a fiery red horse. He is given a large sword and the authority to take peace from the earth. War is clearly intended; people will kill one another as symbolized in the great sword given to him. This bloody warfare is a more universal condition on earth.

The third seal reveals a black horse with a rider holding scales. The scales represent the buying and selling agricultural commodities. The price of the goods mentioned by the voice represents the beginning of scarcity upon the earth. There is a connection here to plight of Egypt in Exodus. Although it is not clearly spelled out in the text, the plagues upon Egypt

---

29. Osborn notes that the plagues, as in God's battle with Egypt, are cosmic both in Egypt and in the book of Revelation (p. 338). Also, the descriptions of power and manifestation are rooted in Sinai. Stern states, "The idea that end times plagues recapitulate those of Egypt is found in Midrash Rabbah. (Exodus Rabbah 12:2) says it will be repeated in the days of God and Magog" (p. 815). So also Bauckham says, "Their content suggest, among many other things, the plagues of Egypt which accompanied the Exodus, the fall of Jericho to the army of Joshua, the army of locusts depicted in the prophecy of Joel, the Sinai theophany, [and] the contemporary fear of invasions by Parthian cavalry" (p. 20).

destroyed crops and livestock, producing famine, scarcity, and death. This weakened Egypt for years and caused her not to be a factor when Israel conquered the land of Canaan.

The fourth seal reveals a pale horse with a rider called Death. Hades (the grave) follows him. He is given power over a fourth of the earth to kill with the sword (war), through hunger (famine), plague (disease), and by the beasts of the earth.[30]

The fifth seal reveals the martyrs. The judgment shown in the martyrs' vision is vengeance for their blood, which will be exacted against those who dwell on the earth. Their saintly robes portray the priestly role of the martyrs. The full number of martyrs includes all from Stephen onward.

There are important implications in these verses. First, the time of vengeance will occur when the suffering of the martyrs is complete (see Chapter 5 about the completion of suffering through the rapture and Chapter 6 about God's wrath unleashed). Paul teaches that believers fill up that which is lacking in the sufferings of the Messiah. The Messiah fully paid the price for everyone's sins, so a believer does not suffer to pay the price for the sins of others. However, a believer's testimony to his death and Resurrection requires suffering, for some even unto death. Some believers suffer to bring the message of Yeshua to the world. Without their witness the Messiah's benefits are not offered to the world. This is what is lacking in the Messiah's suffering, the kind of suffering that results from bringing the gospel to the nations and is the necessary addition to his suffering.

---

30. It is not difficult to see the involvement of principalities, powers, and spiritual warfare in the current famines and shortages in Africa, Russia, and Central America. Devastating wars are one of the great reasons for some of these disasters, as in Ethiopia. These events could be seen as earthly harbingers of heavenly judgment to come.

Second, the witnessing of believers will lead some to repentance and salvation, but it also will lead to the hardening of some hearts and, by extension, to severe consequences. The martyrs' blood releases God's power in both mercy and judgment, depending upon a human's response. The full vengeance of God will come.

During this time, several other fulfillments of prophecy take place. First, the gospel of the Kingdom will be preached throughout the world (Matt. 24:12–14), and a full company from all nations comprises the Bride of the Messiah. I believe that, in spite of the rejection by the majority of the world, *the Church will see its greatest harvest from all of the world's peoples during the Last Days.* This is the "fullness of the Gentiles"(Rom. 11:25). In short, it will be the time of her most powerful witness. It is the final restoration of God's People before the Messiah comes. Lastly, Israel's leaders will call upon Yeshua to save them in their final great war, "Blessed is He who comes in the name of the Lord" (Matt. 23:39).

The sixth seal reveals a great earthquake, the sun becoming dark, the moon becoming as blood, the stars falling from the heavens, the sky rolled up as a scroll, and the mountains and islands shifting.[31] The people described in the sixth seal are not repentant or calling upon God for salvation. So great is this

---

31. Compare this passage with Joel 2:28–32. After the Spirit is poured out, the sun darkens and the moon turns to blood before the great day of God's wrath. Joel has many references in Revelation, even to the final war in the land of Israel described in Revelation 19 in Joel 3. Bauckham notes the connection of the prophecy of Joel 3 in the book of Revelation (p. 20). Also, partial fulfillments of this prophecy were seen when Jesus died on the cross: The sun became dark, and a great earthquake occurred. (Was this a factor in the rending of the veil in the Temple?) However, the ultimate fulfillment of Joel's words concerning the fullness of the Holy Spirit's outpouring in a later reign and God's awesome judgment, still awaits.

cataclysmic judgment that they hide in caves and in the rocks of the mountains, saying:

> "Fall on us and hide us from the face of him who sits on the throne and from the wrath of the Lamb! For the great day of his wrath has come, and who is able to stand?" (Rev. 6:16–17)

Again, the separation between symbolic and literal description is difficult to discern. Earth and heaven still exist after the sixth seal so an eclipse can darken the sun. Volcanic eruptions and earthquakes also can block the sun and make the moon appear to be red. These could be literal interpretations of the plagues. Figuratively, the stars falling could refer to rulers and heavenly principalities, and the description of the sky rolling up like a scroll seems to be symbolic of heavens that disappear from human sight because of these awful judgments. It is well to note that the people described in the sixth seal are not repentant or calling upon God for salvation.

Recall, too, that the darkening of the sun was one of the judgments upon Egypt. It was the next-to-last plague, followed only by the killing of the Egyptian firstborns. This plague initially led to Pharaoh releasing the Israelites from enslavement on the condition that they left their livestock behind. When Moses insisted on the flocks and herds accompanying them, Pharaoh, his heart hardened, refused. Just like in Revelation, Pharaoh's heart was unrelenting and further devastation was exacted upon him and his people.

Revelation 6 ends with the proclamation that the day of God's wrath has come because the seventh seal is ready to be taken from the scroll. This seal includes the seven trumpets and the seven bowls of God's wrath, which are within the seventh trumpet. A specific succession of events follows these symbols. (Revelation 7 was discussed at the beginning of this chapter with the sealing of the 144,000.)

In Revelation 8:1–6 comes *the seventh seal.* This seal reveals the seven angels with seven trumpets (which could be *shofarot,* or rams' horns). An angel with a golden censer offers incense with the saints' prayers upon the golden altar. These prayers ascend before God. Apparently the prayers of the saints affect events in heaven and on earth. Intercession brings God's mighty judgments and redemptive acts. Hence, when the censer is thrown to earth, there are "noises, thundering, lightning, and an earthquake."

The First Six Trumpets (Rev. 8:1–9:21)

The first trumpet produced hail and fire mingled with blood. This plague burned up a third of the trees and all the green grass.[32] This parallels Exodus 9:13–35 when God unleashes a plague of hail on Egypt after Pharaoh refuses to release the Israelites. In Exodus the hail fell as thunder and lightning filled the sky, and it killed anything in its path. The barley and flax crops were completely destroyed; only the wheat and spelt, which had not ripened, survived. The result of both of these plagues is devastation of the vegetation, with the judgment in Revelation extending throughout the earth.

---

32. See Osborn where he also notes that the first trumpet already takes us beyond the Egyptian plagues in intensity and extent, with hail, fire, and blood (p. 350). Again, the parallel plague of water turning to blood is much greater in extent and is a replication of that disaster (p. 353, 354). According to G.R. Beasley-Murray, *The Revelation: New Bible Commentary.* (Grand Rapids, Mich.: Eerdmans, 1970), "the first four Trumpet judgment has distinct reminiscences of the Egyptian plagues" (p. 1291).

When the *second angel sounded his trumpet,* something like a burning mountain was thrown into the sea and a third of the sea became blood. A third of the sea's creatures died, and a third of the ships were destroyed. This parallels the first plague against the Egyptians in Exodus 7:14–24, where God turned all of the water in Egypt to blood, killing the fish and causing the Egyptians to dig wells for fresh water along the Nile. Both plagues infiltrate the seas, poisoning the water and interrupting fishing and shipping enterprises.

The third trumpet reveals a great star, Wormwood, which falls from heaven, burning like a torch. The plague of this trumpet produces bitter waters in the rivers, which cause death.[33] Judgment has been extended from the oceans to the rivers, infecting water supplies and breeding disease.

The fourth trumpet darkens a third of the light of the moon, stars, and sun.[34] The judgment founded on earth has infiltrated the heavens. The fourth trumpet also depicts an angel who cries three woes because of the next three trumpets. As mentioned earlier, the ninth plague in Exodus caused darkness to fall all over Egypt for three days (Ex. 10:21–29), covering the land in darkness.

The fifth trumpet in Revelation 9 allows the angel to release the locusts from the bottomless pit. The sun and air were darkened, both from the number of locusts and from the smoke from the pit. The locusts are described as having a scorpion-like power. The locusts are given authority to torment men for five months with a torment like a scorpion sting. The description of

---

33. Keener notes that the bitter waters parallel the water of *marah* (Ex. 15:23) but with the opposite conclusion (p. 256).

34. Osborn notes that the fourth judgment replicates the ninth Egyptian plague where darkness covers the earth (p. 355).

the locusts—shaped like horses, heads with crowns of gold, and faces like men—indicate that this is more than an insect plague made up of a strange type of stinging locust. The amazing description of this plague continues in Revelation 9:8–10. The king of the locusts is the angel of the bottomless pit, Abaddon, the destroyer. As mentioned earlier in this chapter, they harm only those men who do not have the seal of God on their heads. Here it is specifically noted that *God distinguishes his People from the people of the world and protects them.* Just as the Israelites in Egypt, God's People are not subject to the plagues.

The parallel to the Exodus is clear in the plague of locusts (Ex. 10:1–20).[35] God sent the locusts to Egypt after Pharaoh's heart remained hard, and he refused to humble himself before God. They descended upon the land and devoured the crops remaining after the plague of hail. In Exodus the plague is limited to the ravishing the fields and foliage. However, in Revelation this plague is worldwide and intensified.

In Revelation 9:6, it says men will seek death and not find it. They are afraid to live and afraid to die. Yet, just as the Egyptians did, they do not repent and turn to the living God. Their hearts are just as hard as pharaoh's was.

The sixth trumpet (Rev. 9:13–21) sounds, and John hears a voice from the golden altar[36] saying, "Release the four angels who are bound at the great river Euphrates" (v. 14). These angels are released to kill a third of mankind. There is also an incredible army on horses. The riders have breastplates of fiery red, blue,

---

35. For Osborn the locusts replicate the eighth Egyptian plague (p. 364).

36. Throughout Revelation, there are parallels to Hebrews. In the latter book the Tabernacle of old is symbolic of spiritual realities in heaven, the heavenly Tabernacle. In Revelation there is the altar, censer, golden altar, and other pictures of the reality of God and his place of abode.

and yellow. The horses have heads of lions and breathe fire and smoke, and they do harm with their mouths and tails. The number of people killed would be more than 1.5 billion today. Amazingly, those not killed still do not repent of their ways:

> [T]hat they should not worship demons, and idols of gold, silver, brass, stone, and wood, which can neither see nor hear nor walk; and they did not repent of their murders or their sorceries or their sexual immoralities or their thefts. (Rev. 9:20–21)

The Meaning Behind the Trumpets' Judgment

Once again, these events stemming from trumpets could be literal—as in large meteors falling to earth (second and third trumpets); the aftereffects of earthquakes and volcanic eruptions, nuclear wars, or a combination of the two (fourth trumpet); or a plague of locusts (fifth trumpet).Or the trumpets could also be a means of describing what is unseen but has effects on the seen world. For example, the judgment of the fifth trumpet—the locusts—could be demonic hosts released by God to torment men because they refused to turn to him. God could use these demonic hosts, which are under his authority, as instruments of the world's judgment. In regard to the sixth trumpet, the hosts on horseback could refer to awesome demonic powers, which seek to destroy mankind but are still under God's control and limitations. God uses their desire to destroy as part of his arm of judgment. It is well to leave the full meaning to God. The description goes beyond what can be identified in human terms.

Some of the judgments from the trumpets could even be linked to aspects currently seen in the world. For example, a limited fulfillment of the fourth trumpet is unveiled in water pollution, which produces death rapidly in some Third World environments or leads to disease and poor health in many advanced parts of the world. In the aftermath of the sixth trumpet some have seen the cavalcade as a literal reference to huge armies, such as China's military, that come from beyond the Euphrates (the east). Modern military vehicles, like tanks, which "sting" from the head and tail, could appear like this in a vision, especially to someone of John's time.

In our present experience, God's judgments produce anger among many but not repentance. People debate the problem of evil and ask how a good God could allow such evil to fall upon mankind. Yet mankind is not in the full favor of God's protection; the world is plagued—under judgment for sin. God does not see man as the "good guys." A look at plagues and disasters throughout history, especially today, indicates that they do not usually bring men to repent before a holy God. The AIDS plague, other venereal diseases, famines, and disasters are the result of gross sin, greed, shortsightedness, and hatred in the human race. Yet, God is blamed for the judgments that humanity brings upon itself. Surely the picture of these verses from Revelation is even now sad and accurate.

CHAPTER FOUR

The Persecution

The discussion of the theme of the anti-Messiah,
the Last Days' Pharaoh, stems from texts in
Revelation 10; 11:1–10; 13; 17; and 18:1–19.

As noted earlier, the progression of events in the Book of Revelation is best followed by studying the succession of the seals, trumpets, and bowls. However, between the depictions of these judgments are excursuses, passages containing more detailed descriptions of the Last Days, which interrupt the progression. They give insight into the nature of the whole period or expand on one aspect of it, as do the chapters from Revelation referenced in this chapter. Here the focus is on the several excursuses that denote the persecution inflicted on the body of believers. These events happen in concert with the judgments discussed in Chapter 3.

The Inflictors of the Persecution During the Plagues (Rev. 13; 17–18)

In the midst of the judgments brought down on mankind, the Book of Revelation presents a picture of the End Times leaders who oppose and persecute the People of God. There is rich imagery here. The central figure of these leaders is the anti-Messiah, represented by the form of a grotesque beast. His response to God's People is similar to the response of Pharaoh to the Israelites in Egypt. Revelation also provides symbolism for Satan, the Devil, in the form of the dragon; the false prophet to contrast the two righteous prophets mentioned in Revelation 11; the harlot, the image of false religion; and Babylon, the image of the ungodly kingdom. These beacons of evil relentlessly pursue the saints until death and that persecution leads to the completion of the martyrs. This is the darkest aspect of the tribulation, but as has been seen throughout Revelation, God does not abandon his People and is present with them even during this time.

The Beast from the Sea: the Last Days Pharaoh (Rev. 13:1–10)

The fact that the beast comes from the sea is symbolic of his arising from the peoples (Rev. 13:1). Its seven heads and ten horns are reminiscent of the Book of Daniel (chapter 7). Seven is the number of perfection and ten of completeness. This is the perfect completeness of evil rule. Again, the ten horns could represent authority over nations centered in either ten symbolic or literal nations. The beast is swift like a leopard and strong like a bear; he boasts authority as a lion roars. His power and authority come from the dragon, Satan.

Not only do the people worship the beast, but also they directly worship Satan, the dragon, who gives power to the beast. The fact that the beast boasts great things (as did ancient pharaohs and other Middle-Eastern kings) harkens to the little horn who so boasts in Daniel 7. Again, many rulers fit the description of Daniel 7, beginning with Antiochus IV in the second century, BCE. The beast blasphemes, or speaks in boastful terms, concerning his position while coming against that which is holy or of God. Again, the time frame is forty-two months (three and one half years) for his dominating rule.

The parallel to Pharaoh is based in the basic understanding of anti-Messiah figures. The general characteristics are tyrants who have great political power on earth, oppose God, and oppress the People of God. Such figures also seek worship from their subjects. Pharaoh is the first in the line of such figures in the Bible and the anti-Messiah is the last.

Although the Devil and those given to him—including the anti-Messiah—engage the saints in war, both spiritually and physically, all such tests are ultimately under the control of God for the purification of the body. The beast is given authority to make war and to overcome the saints. This does not, in my view, mean that he ultimately destroys the body of believers, but that his campaign of persecution leads to the martyrdom of many saints and his *apparent* victory over the saints. There also will be a *full* revelation of evil in the anti-Messiah, his false occult religious system, and economic tyranny (2 Thessalonians 2). During his violent oppression, the Bride of the Messiah will come to maturity, or completeness, in unity, love, and power before she will join Yeshua (John 17:24).

Verses 7–8 tell us that the beast achieves great world domination over every "tribe, tongue, and nation." Humanity is divided into two: those whose names are written in the Lamb's Book of Life and all others. Yet verse 10 assures us that God's judgment will ultimately prevail. The law of sowing and reaping will prove true. Confidence in God will produce "patience and the faith of the saints" (v. 9).

The Identity of the Beast, Part 1

Many have speculated concerning the identity of the beast. (Because of the finality of these chapters in Revelation, I believe God must give more light during the events yet to come for any conclusions to be made.) Some have been prompted to see this in terms of a literal Roman emperor, with the seven heads being a succession of emperors. Thus, the beast is not one ruler, but a succession of rulers of the same spirit. The one wounded is either the last in the series or one of the series. Prophetic speculators have also sought to identify just the wounded head, with the beast's heads representing different people. Some have seen the wounded head as prophetic of Hitler's injury after the bomb attack that failed to kill him. Some have even seen it manifested in the near-fatal wound suffered by Pope John Paul II after the attempt upon his life, even though the injury was not on his head. Paul makes it clear in 2 Thessalonians 2 that there will be an ultimate world ruler designated "anti-Messiah." Do they marvel at the beast because of a healing from the wound? The text is not clear, but this is possible.

A great deal of speculation is given as well by those who believe that these texts should be seen as primarily related to the first century. The text's symbolism, including the seven hills mentioned, fits the Roman Empire. Many as well see the figure in terms of Nero. The number 666 has been shown to add up to the numeric value of the letters of his name. A common Roman fear was that Nero somehow survived and that the mad emperor would return, perhaps leading a Parthian army from the East, so that he could conquer Rome. However, most do not believe that the book of Revelation was written soon after the time of Nero. Rather, the broadest consensus is that it was written during the days of Domitian, which was also a period of persecution in some regions of the empire. As noted, the text was relevant to the people of that day, so these speculations have merit. However, I believe the text will be greatly relevant to the people on earth just before the Second Coming of the Messiah.[37]

The False Prophet (Rev. 13:11–17)

After the anti-Messiah emerges from the sea, a second beast arises from the land. His two horns symbolize strength or authority. It is possible that they represent a double portion of authority, or there may be two prophets carrying the leadership of false prophets. There will be many false prophets in the Last Days.[38]However, just as the people of God are represented in two prominent prophets (Rev. 11), paralleling Moses and Aaron in ancient Egypt, so this beast represents false prophets of the Last Days. As did the false prophets of Pharaoh, this beast performs signs. But his signs are much greater than those performed by the magicians of Egypt. He can call fire from heaven and do such stupendous signs that the world remains deceived and does not repent when the true prophets speak

---

37.   Osborn surmises that Nero is the most likely candidate for the symbol of 666 (p. 521). However, Osborn does not think that Nero is the literal figure designated as the anti-Messiah. He is rather an image of anti-Messiah. Osborn notes the Roman fear that the kings of the East would turn against Rome and a Nero revived myth (p. 620–630). Keener sees the beast as one like Nero and shows the expectation for such a great beast (p. 337). The consensus is that the book was written in the 90s during the time of Domitian. This does not mean that Domitian is the literal beast.

38.   The New Age movement provides a picture of a subtle but sinister religious movement with its own cadre of false prophets.

truth through plagues, signs, and wonders.[39]He prophesies to the nations to encourage them to worship the first beast, the anti-Messiah. Signs and wonders are vividly described:

> He performs great signs, so that he even makes fire come down from heaven on the earth in the sight of men. And he deceives those who dwell on the earth by those signs which he was granted to do in the sight of the beast, telling those who dwell on the earth to make an image to the beast who was wounded by the sword and lived. (Rev. 13:13–14)

This beast even causes the idol of the first beast to speak and has those who do not worship the anti-Messiah killed. Similar to a robot-like figure, he can give the orders for execution. This worship is professed by taking upon the mark of the beast, the human anti-Messiah ruler. The mark is required for economic transactions.[40]

The Meaning Behind the Number 666

The number of the beast is 666. Great attempts have been made to find emperors or contemporary figures whose names

---

39. Many have noted the parallel to the Exodus. Keener briefly notes the false signs as parallel to Exodus 7:11 (p. 352). Stern notes that the false prophet deceives as the false magicians during the Exodus story at the court of pharaoh (p. 828). Also he points to the fire from heaven as a false sign parallel to the Elijah miracle (1 Kings 18). Bauckham points to a satanic trinity of the dragon, beast, and false prophet (p. 84).

40. Keener notes that the mark of the beast is in contrast to the seal of believers in Revelation 7 (p. 352). Ancient societies had marks and incisions for slaves and religious rituals. Even so, God's People are instructed in the Torah to bind his Law on their heads and hands. However, modern computer technology has rightly caused some to think that this could imply new and more frightening dimensions in the Last Days.

have this numerical value. Nero is the likely historical figure fitting 666, but he is a symbolic figure pointing to a final anti-Messiah.[41] The number 666 is also the first part of the numeric series of today's bar codes, which are used in computer scanning in many transactions. Surely these are possibilities in our computerized society. However, the speculations for specific identifications have yielded little fruit. The number six in Hebrew numerology is the number of man. Multiplied by three, it is a representation of man apart from God, building his own kingdom and authority; three sixes are the false human trinity, seeking to replace the triune God.

The Scarlet Woman, the Beast, and the Fall of Babylon (Rev. 17–18)

The final passage concerning the representatives of evil during the End Times begins in Revelation 17. Revelation 17 and 18 give an expanded picture of what God's People are up against in the Last Days with a clear prophecy of the defeat of the forces of evil. It describes a scarlet woman sitting on a beast who appears similar to the first beast of Revelation 13. The woman is arrayed with great jewels. She is "Mystery, Babylon the Great, the Mother of Harlots and of the abominations of the earth" (Rev. 17:5). This woman is drunk with the blood of the martyrs. She is the representation of religious, economic, and political power conjoined into one ungodly world system.

---

41. Osborn gives a summary of the options and agrees that Nero is the historical basis for the symbol (p. 521).

The Identity of the Beast, Part 2

Further information is given here about the first beast from Revelation 13. Its seven heads represent the seven hills, a clear reference to Rome. Roman power, at the time of Revelation, was the Babylonian system of the day. The seven kings represent the succession of ungodly emperors. The seventh has not yet come (v. 10).

The numbers become complex here. Are we speaking of a succession of known emperors during the first century? Many have thought so and have tried to give identifications. Yet the focus of the book ultimately stretches beyond the first century to the very end of this transitional age. Aneighth head is described that arises out of the seventh. Is this none other than the final representative of the whole series? I believe it is. The ten horns represent lesser rulers who control various kingdoms under the beast. By supporting the beast they give him power and authority.

A Deeper View of the Overcoming of the Saints

Revelation 13 explains that the beast makes war against the saints and overcomes them. However, this is an incomplete picture as evidenced in Revelation 17. The saints are joined to the Messiah Yeshua. Ultimately, the beast's war against the saints is war against the Messiah.[42]

> These [kings] will make war with the Lamb, and
> the Lamb will overcome them, for he is Lord of
> lords and King of kings; and those who are with
> him are called, chosen, and faithful. (Rev. 17:14)

---

42. For Bauckham, the martyrdom of the saints is their victory (p. 71). That the beast overcomes the saints is paradoxically the release of the power that leads to the defeat of the beast.

The Scarlet Woman's Role

The harlot sits over the waters, representing "peoples, multi-tudes, nations, and tongues." This whole evil system—the beast (anti-Messiah) and harlot (chief city of the world)—becomes dominant over the earth just before the last battle. Strangely, verse 17 tells us that the ten kings will hate the harlot, make her desolate, and "eat her flesh and burn her with fire."[43] The woman is a harlot because she is the image of spiritual adultery, or unfaithfulness to God the Father. The woman is described as the chief city of the world system (v. 18). I believe this refers to the fact that the rulers of this world, as well as rulers of the false system, have within themselves the seeds of their own destruction.[44]

The announcement of the contamination of the false city and its system of evil is a source of rejoicing for the saints. A bright angel with great authority announces the destruction (Rev. 18:1–2). The description of Babylon, the great harlot, is clearly a full description of decadence:

> "Babylon the great is fallen, is fallen, and has become a habitation of demons, a prison for every foul spirit, and a cage for every unclean and hated bird! For all of the nations have drunk

---

43. Osborn explains the beast and kings turning against Jezebel is connected to the Roman fear of kings turning against Rome and a Nero revived myth (p. 620–630). I point to the fact that Nero burned Rome and really was very destructive to the empire. Eventually evil rulers destroy the societies they rule.

44. Some have seen contemporary New York from 1970 to 1990 as a good representation of the false kingdoms of this world. They see the humanist systems, the perversions, and the initiatives taken in this city as having perverted the whole country. The city itself could be deemed as rotting through the seeds of destruction inherent in its false philosophies and behaviors.

of the wine of the wrath of her fornication, the kings of the earth have committed fornication with her, and the merchants of the earth have become rich through the abundance of her luxury." (Rev. 18:2–3)

God's People are called to come out of her (v. 4). Believers are to be separate from the world system, living according to the holy standards of God by the power of the Spirit. This call to holiness is necessary to avoid the plagues of God's judgments and receive his protection. Carnal, worldly, compromising "believers" will not be protected from the plagues of the Last Days. Verses 7–8 make it clear that the judgment on the harlot will be swift. She will be burned by fire.

Revelation 18:21–24 predicts the fall of the Babylonian system in terms of the fall of a city. A literal city may indeed fall, but the destruction of the whole system is the central issue. As a millstone thrown into the sea, so will Babylon fall,with violence. She shall be found no more. All the sounds of social life and industry will fully cease. The description is striking.

And the light of a lamp shall not shine in you anymore. And the voice of bridegroom and bride shall not be heard in you anymore. For your merchants were the great men of the earth, for by your sorcery all the nations were deceived. And in her was found the blood of prophets and saints, and of all who were slain on the earth. (Rev. 18:23–24)

The Mighty Angel and the Little Book (Rev. 10:1–11)

With evil rampant throughout the world and the persecution of believers in full force, the climactic battleground for the persecution is set, pointing to the completion of the body of believers. In Revelation 10 a mighty angel appears, descending from heaven. This angel in Revelation is variously interpreted. Some have seen the figure as the Messiah because the description of his majesty is so great. The rainbow present in the account is a covenant sign, and the fact that the angel is "clothed with a [glory] cloud" corresponds to the revelation of God in the pillar of cloud to Moses and the children of Israel in Exodus. When the angel speaks, seven thunders, like the roar of a lion, resound. (Seven, again, is the number of perfection. Thunder is a description of the voice of God; the roar of a lion connotes kingship.) Like the biblical imagery in Psalm 29, the voice of the Lord is powerful upon many waters. The angel of Revelation 10 stands with a foot on the land and a foot on the sea, a sign of ample authority over all the earth. Of course, the identification with the Messiah is not absolutely certain because other passages in Revelation identify the Messiah outright. Hence scholars are quite divided on this question.

Most significant is Revelation 10:7, which says by the sounding of the seventh angel of the seventh trumpet, "The mystery of God would be finished, as he declared to his servants the prophets." I believe this mystery is the completion of the Bride of the Messiah. In Pauline writings the mystery of the Church is revealed that Jew and Gentile are to be one body in the Messiah *before the actual full establishment of the worldwide Kingdom of the Messiah.[45] The first-century Jews looked for a specific order to End Time events, and the apostles shared much of this perspective. My view is that before Acts 9, the apostles believed in this order of the Last Days: First, Israel would repent and turn to the Messiah, and then he would deliver Israel from all her enemies. Only after this would the world see the truth and approach God. Then all of the world would be one in faith as Zechariah 14:9 proclaims and all of the prophets predicted.*

Paul's great revelation in the Spirit was that God was, during Paul's time, taking out of every nation a representative people who would constitute his ruling Bride. They would be his resurrected rulers in the Age to Come. The Bride foreshadows the Age to Come, in which Israel and the nations will be one under Yeshua's rule. To complete the Bride of the Messiah, I believe, implies that both every nation has entered the Kingdom and the People of God have come into unity, power, and holiness. This is the implication of Yeshua's prayer for the unity of his People in John 17. Paul also teaches this in Ephesians 4, where he says that the fivefold ministry will equip the saints until they come to the full maturity of the Messiah. Revelation 10:7 clearly indicates that the body of the Messiah is on earth during the Great Tribulation until the seventh trumpet. This verse also hints at the forthcoming rapture of the saints (see Chapter 5).

John is told to eat the little book that is in the angel's hand. It is sweet in his mouth but bitter in his stomach. The

---

45. Stern adds to this and asserts that the mystery is the plan of God, the Kingdom, and all it entails (p. 818). However, I would add that the completion of the Church in number and task is central to the coming of the fullness of the Kingdom.

conclusion of the passage (v. 11) says that John will prophesy about many peoples, nations, tongues, and kings. This indicates that to channel God's word is indeed sweet, but the messages of judgment are hard for the prophet to receive and deliver.

The Two Witnesses (Rev. 11:1–10)

After eating the book, John is commanded to measure the Temple. The court is to be left out because it is given to the Gentiles (all nations). It is said that the Gentiles will tread the holy city under foot for forty-two months. The language here parallels Luke 21, which says that Gentiles will tread down Jerusalem until their time is complete. Is this the final act and manifestation of the decline, or is this a reinstatement of Gentile control? Many students of prophecy believe that Luke 21 was fulfilled when Jerusalem was captured in 1967. However, Israel has left the Temple Mount in Arab control for political and religious reasons. Some see here a reference to pagan infiltration into the Church. However, I believe this is a reference to Israel's national struggles in the Last Days.[46]

Some believe John's measuring the Temple implies the

---

46. Bauckham sees such things as references to apocalyptic time (p. 87). It is not to be taken literally although the parallel in Daniel is probably literal and taken from the time of the Maccabean war against the Syrian-Greeks and their control of Jerusalem and the Temple. However, a literal time of trial in the final End Times is still possible. To extend the time of forty-two months, or three and a half years, to cover the course of world history is a bit of a stretch in spite of the symbolic nature of the text. Bauckham does allow that the three and a half years shows the onslaught's intensity at the end. He notes that the Church is called to provoke and win the conflict by preserving faithful witness. I have argued as well that a faithful, restored Church provokes the events of the Last Days. Note as well that for interpreters like Bauckham the Jerusalem and Temple references are symbolic of the Church as a whole. Keener also stretches the three and a half years as symbolic of the Church Age and the witness of the Church (p. 286–296). He leans very much to the symbolic tradition of interpretation.

existence of a literal Temple during this time and see a parallel in 2 Thessalonians 2, where the anti-Messiah shall sit in the Temple of God and blaspheme. Yet because the body of believers is also called the Temple of God, it would be wise to wait until prophetic fulfillments make this clear. The focus of Revelation should be less for speculation and more for the preparation of the Second Coming and the understanding of present warfare. Measuring the Temple could relate to examining God's People or the area of the Holy City, which is in view.

The description of the two witnesses that follows is most important. The conditions of the Last Days are very similar to those of the Roman Empire. There is a world of opposition to the gospel, the Jewish people again are in their Land, and there is great warfare between the Church and the forces of darkness. These men prophesy for 1,260 days—or three and a half years on the lunar 360-day year. These witnesses have the power to "shut Heaven," that is, to speak drought into existence, turn water into blood, and strike the earth with all kinds of plagues as often as they desire. This power correlates to the plagues mentioned in the previous chapter. Note that the plagues of Revelation do not randomly happen to mankind; rather, they occur as a result of prophetic speaking. The world will have prophetic warning before the great plagues occur—another way God will protect his People. This is a great key to Revelation's nature.

Just who are the two witnesses? This situation will be reminiscent of ancient Egypt when Moses and Aaron announced the plagues and judgments upon the Egyptians. Some have theorized that they are Enoch and Elijah who have come back to earth because they never physically died, but following their return, the two prophets will die. This is one possibility. Others have thought these will be two leading prophets of the Last Days, one representing the Jews and the other the Gentiles. Some have thought that the two represent the ministries of the prophet and the apostle, which God is restoring in these Last Days. The two witnesses could either be a literal leading apostle and a prophet, or they could simply be symbolic of the restoration of these ministries.[47] All of these are good possibilities.

I personally believe there will be two literal prophets in Jerusalem in the Last Days, but that these two prophets represent the gift of prophecy being restored all over the world, similar to the first century and the Old Testament period. Kings and presidents will be called to take heed. They will tremble at the words of God from the Last Days' prophets. However, this does not mean that the world will repent. During this time there will be many prophets in the body of the Messiah. They will give guidance to the Last Days' Church for waging spiritual war and announce judgments to the nations. Gifts of great authority and empowerment for ministry, as implied in

---

47. Osborn notes that the two witnesses are Moses and Elijah figures (p. 422). He notes that Moses has power to turn water to blood (p. 423). The Egyptian plagues are replicated by the two witnesses (p. 424). Keener is sympathetic to the idea of Moses and Elijah or Enoch and Elijah and points to Jewish sources (p. 286–296). Stern emphasizes the Moses' background in calling down plagues and striking the earth (p. 820). Bauckham sees the two witnesses as representing the Church (p. 84, 85). Two is a legal category for adequate witness. The witnesses are modeled on the roles of Moses and Elijah. However, unlike Moses and Elijah and like Yeshua, they suffer martyrdom, so for Bauckham, the symbol of the Church's suffering believers, like Yeshua, is added to the meaning. Gilmore also connects the two witnesses to Zerubbabel and Joshua (p. 958). Beasley-Murray sees the two witnesses as the missionary activity of the whole Church (p. 1293). John identifies Rome with Egypt and Jerusalem with Sodom, showing that Jew and Gentile combine to crush the faithful witness of believers (p. 1993).

Ephesians 4:11–16 and Yeshua's prayer in John 17, will be evident. The restoration of prophets continues today,[48] but it has not yet come to the power and prominence described in Revelation 11.

The guidance of the body of believers is also important. The worldwide Church in the Last Days will follow these apostles and prophets. They will tell believers to leave cities before bombs drop, earthquakes hit, or plagues are poured out so that God's People can be protected. Some reject this stress on prophetic guidance because all believers have the Spirit and can receive guidance from God. However, I believe that is too individualistic. I believe that because all true believers have the indwelling of Holy Spirit, inner confirmation becomes very important. *Those with pure and humble hearts will verify the guidance from God's true prophets.* Believers are a corporate body, and there will be corporate leadership for congregations. God speaks to his corporate body through his captains. Individuals will not receive the revelation for the body, but they will receive it through leadership. If inner pride blocks that view of corporate leading from the apostles and prophets, lives will be endangered in the Last Days. The body will have to learn to move as God's spiritual army in discipline and rank. Confirmation will be important but so will knowing who is

---

48. One example is the 1989 San Francisco earthquake. There were prophets of God who predicted the quake. It occurred on the first day of baseball's World Series while the nation looked on via television. Before the first pitch was thrown, the quake struck. Although there was some loss of life, the quake was not catastrophic. Prophets of stature and credibility had not yet become known; thus, there was no recognized voice announcing the coming judgment and no later public interpretation. When the Last Days' plagues and judgments occur, public prediction will precede the judgments. People will have a prophetic context through which to perceive that the events are judgments from God and repentance will be their responsibility.

trustworthy and can be followed. Believers will not always have days to confirm whether the word is from the Lord. Hearts will need to be so humble and pure that immediately believers can bear witness to the true leading of God's apostles and prophets and know those called to lead through the battles. This will be part of the way Jesus will purify his Church. *As mentioned earlier in Chapter 2, the key preparations for the Last Days are a holy heart, humble demeanor, burning love for the Lord, and faith rooted in the Word that will serve as a guide to God's counsel and strength to withstand the enemy's onslaught.*

The two witnesses are finally overcome by the beast from the pit (the anti-Messiah) and killed. God's holy people can be martyred only when he calls upon them to lay down their lives. When believers are free of sin, they have his great protection even through the times of Revelation. The prophets are supernaturally protected from all who desire to harm them. Fire proceeds from their mouths and devours their enemies. I believe this means the words of God from their mouths produce fiery judgments. This raises the question of the extent of God's protection during these difficult days.

I believe that as Yeshua said, that no one had power over him, but that he would lay down his life, so is the situation with the two witnesses and the various segments of the restored body of the Messiah in the Last Days. Believers will be fully protected in many ways: in Goshens of God, or protected cities; through supernatural acts of God; and in many other ways. Remember when people sought to kill Yeshua; either supernatural power or circumstances from God prevented them. Yet there was a point at which God desired that Yeshua lay down his life. As Yeshua taught, in the ultimate sense, not a hair of a believer's head will be lost. However, in the proximate sense, some will be called upon by God to lay down their lives.

After the murder of the two witnesses, the wicked hearts of the world's people are then revealed because they rejoice and give gifts to one another. Instead of repenting, they are glad that the ones for whom they blamed the plagues are dead. Rather than seeing their torment as God's judgment, the world will have its own interpretation. In some fashion they will see their religious philosophy triumphing over the prophets of God and will now expect peace, "Get rid of the believers and all shall be well!" The anti-Messiah will be allowed to temporarily triumph over the body of believers, just like the crafty magicians in Egypt were able to replicate the first two plagues God brought down on Egypt.[49] It seemed to the Israelites that they were being overcome by Pharaoh and their slave masters and for a time their slavery was made worse!

For three and a half days the two prophets' bodies lie in the city, figuratively called Sodom and Egypt,[50] where the Lord was crucified. This could be a reference to Last Days' Jerusalem. Until the Jewish leadership turns to Yeshua, they will make compromises with the anti-Messiah even against believers.

---

49. For example, such an overcoming took place through Adolf Hitler and Germany as they unleashed the Holocaust during World War II.

50. This indicates the spiritual depravity and stubbornness of the people. Sodom was known for its debauchery and sinful ways in Genesis. Egypt, as has been mentioned earlier, was known for its hardness of heart in Exodus. Both experienced the wrath and judgment of God.

The State of the Body of Believers Toward the End of the Persecution

Although the anti-Messiah has an apparent victory over the saints during the tribulation, it is clear that the victory of the saints is assured. Although circumstances will look dark, the spiritual reality will be that the saved from all nations will be more purified, unified, and empowered than they have been since the first century. The purity and unity of God's People is expressed through intense intercession. Having completed its gospel witness, been a light to Israel, endured intense suffering and persecution, God's People will stand in a position similar to that of the children of Israel before they crossed the Red Sea.

As the Israelites at the sea seemed to be defeated by the advancing forces of Pharaoh, so the body of believers will seem crushed by the anti-Messiah's forces in the Last Days. A worldwide attack will be advancing upon them, and Israel will also see an invasion by the anti-Messiah's forces. As Zechariah 14 states, all nations will come upon Jerusalem. Half of the city will go into exile; their women will be raped; destruction from the forces of the anti-Messiah will be upon the city. It will look dark indeed for both Israel and the body of Christ.

CHAPTER FIVE

The Exodus Rapture

*The theme of the Exodus rapture is found
in Revelation 11:11–19 and 14:1–16.*

A good overall metaphor for the Last Days is the World
Series in baseball. The end of the Last Days is the seventh
game of the series. The overcoming by the beast (Revelation
13) is his lead in that final, deciding game. The score is 6–3.
The home team, the body of believers, is at the plate with two
outs. Through the power of the Spirit, the Church will get a
hit, walk, and bunt single. The bases are loaded. It is at this
moment that Satan, on the mound, faces the Player–Manager
Yeshua the Messiah. Yeshua comes to bat and hits a grand slam
for victory. As the home team's runners circle the bases and
touch home plate, the team has been changed into champions
and will never be the same again.

In Revelation at this point, the situation for believers is
that crucial ninth inning in the seventh game. It is dark and all
hope seems gone. But for believers in Yeshua, this situation
will be such a clear fulfillment of biblical prophecy. There
still is hope and there will be an unheard of unified cry of
intercession. Believers from every nation will cry out,
"*Maranatha* (Come, Lord)!" for Yeshua's return. I believe

they will also yearn for the salvation and deliverance of Israel. This unity of holiness, faith, and intercession will be met by the glorious appearing of the Lord Yeshua. Just as Israel was hemmed in by the sea and Moses responded in faith, so, too, will the body of believers be surrounded and put their hope in their God. God must rescue them—just as he did when he parted the Red Sea (Ex. 14:13–14).[51]

The ninth inning hits that load the bases are the body of believers completes its worldwide witness to the Kingdom of God (mentioned in Rev. 10:7 and Chapter 4); through the witness and prayer of believers, including the saved remnant of Israel, Israel considers calling on Yeshua as the key to her salvation; and finally Israel calls upon the Name of Yeshua! Israel's leaders will say, "Blessed is he who comes in the Name of the Lord" (Matt. 23:39). With these three events concluded, Yeshua can return and create a path for believers to travel from earth to heaven and escape the intensifying wrath to come. The rapture of the saints has come.

The phrase "rapture of the saints" has produced significant controversy. This is because some who do not believe in a pre-tribulation rapture (seven years before Yeshua actually comes to earth) think the term *rapture* means "pre-tribulation rapture." It does not; it simply refers to believers being "caught up" to meet the Lord at his coming. In this sense, all believers I know believe in the rapture.

---

51. Osborn states, "It is common to stress the Exodus typology with the victorious saints as Israel who passed through the sea to the other side. However, it is not the sea here per se, but the exchaton as a new Exodus and the deliverance of God's people" (p. 562). As we will see in further notes, other scholars see the Exodus theme sometimes parallel to the rapture theme in different texts.

The Events Leading up to the Rapture

The passage concerning the two witnesses (Rev. 11:1–14) precedes the passage on the blowing of the seventh trumpet (Rev. 11:15–19), and there is some debate as to whether the resurrection of the two prophets occurs as separate or a part of the rapture. Although Revelation is not consistently chronological, I sense that it is better to see this excursus as preceding the rapture because it comes between the blowing of the sixth and seventh trumpets. There is a logic in the placement of the excursus passages that has some relationship to chronology. Some, especially among those who see the witnesses as symbolic of God's People and not as individuals,[52] have seen this resurrection as signaling the rapture of the saints. Although I see the two witnesses as representatives of Last Days' prophets, it seems likely that the world could focus on two leading prophets. This resurrection might even be a sign that pushes Israel toward calling out to Yeshua, "Blessed is he who comes in the Name of the Lord!" (Matt. 23:39), one of the conditions that must be meet for the completion of the body of believers.

The resurrection of the two witnesses could be a resurrection that anticipates the full resurrection of the dead and the transfiguration of the saints. If the passage is

---

52. Bauckham again sees the progression of events as I do (p. 84). The allusions to the final climax, with the resurrection and the transformation of the saints on earth who are caught up, can therefore be alluded to in several passages because Revelation is only broadly consecutive but is also overlapping throughout chapters 11–15 (p. 84, 85). Bauckham, in seeing the witnesses as other commentators, sees their resurrection and ascension as symbolic for the Church.

an excursus, a digressive non-chronological section[53] that somewhat overlaps what follows after the seventh trumpet, then this could be an event that occurs simultaneously with the rapture. In either case, the resurrection of the prophets is an extraordinary sign for introducing the rapture and resurrection of the saints.

The Resurrection of the Two Prophet Witnesses (Rev. 11:11–14)

One sign that the tide has turned involves the two prophets mentioned in the previous chapter. These witnesses were silenced by the beast—killed for their faith. Their death seems to spell doom for the remaining body of believers as the world continues to relentlessly persecute the Church. But after three and a half days, God breathes life back into the two witnesses and they stand on their feet, causing all to fear. The resurrection of the two witnesses is not an instant translation to heaven, because they will stand on their feet and great fear will fall on those who see them. Then a voice will call them into the glory cloud, "Come up here." Their enemies will watch.[54]

---

53. Bauckham is optimistic and sees the passage (Rev. 11:13), indicating the nations turning to faith (p. 87). See also the optimism of Osborn, who sees the conversion of the nations in the same verses (p. 391). Also, the seventh trumpet is the end of world history, as we know it (p. 400). The mystery is complete, and that mystery is the whole of God's plan. Beasley-Murray sees the resurrection as either a tremendous world revival or the rapture of the saints (p. 1294, 1993).

54. As the seventh trumpet sounds, the two witnesses are resurrected, heralding the Second Coming, resurrection of the saints, and the translation of believers in Yeshua. Stern sees that the spiritual condition is such that Jerusalem is like Sodom, and before the resurrection of the two prophets, the Messianic Jews are persecuted (p. 821, 822). Bauckham also sees the activity of the two witnesses in part modeled on Moses and the plagues of Egypt, and one of the prophetic names of the city where they are martyred is Egypt (p. 71). This is connected to the general resurrection. Osborn does not see the resurrection here but at Armageddon, just before the sixth bowl (p. 432).

This is followed by the great earthquake, in which a tenth of the city will fall. This earthquake might parallel the one described in Zechariah 14, in which the Jewish people escape the End Time siege of Jerusalem. If this prophecy is to be fulfilled in a literal fashion, the saints will know that their rapture is at hand. This also could be the beginning of tremors that will eventually lead to the splitting of the Mount of Olives as part of the events that take place at Yeshua's Second Coming (Zech. 14). Zechariah 14 also foreshadows that after that earthquake, the Lord will come with all his saints to fully defeat the forces of the Anti-Messiah.

Who gives glory to God in these events (Rev. 11:13)? Could this be Jewish people who now turn to the Messiah? Could it be the Church, which soon will follow the witnesses into the glory cloud? Could this be some of the peoples of the world who now see the truth and are beginning to turn to Jesus? All of these, in part or combination, are possibilities.

Revelation 11:15–19 returns us to the progression of trumpets, the seventh and final trumpet, which leads to the rapture of the saints and the most awesome judgments upon the world who killed the prophets of God. It is, in my view, the same as the last trumpet foretold in 1 Thessalonians 4:16–17 and 1 Corinthians 15:51–52. Thus, it is the announcement of full triumph.

The Sounding of the Seventh Trumpet (Rev. 11:15–19)

Scripture tells us that the rapture of the saints will occur at the blowing of the last trumpet (1 Cor. 15:51–53, 1 Thess. 4:16–18). The sounding of the seventh trumpet in Revelation 11:10 is very possibly the same as the last trumpet in the other mentioned passages. It heralds the ultimate victory of God and his People:

> Then the seventh angel sounded: And there were loud voices in heaven, saying, "The kingdoms of this world have become the kingdoms of our Lord and of his Christ, and he shall reign forever and ever!" And the twenty-four elders who sat before God on their thrones fell on their faces and worshiped God, saying: "We give you thanks, O Lord God Almighty, the One who is and who was and who is to come, because you have taken your great power and reigned. The nations were angry, and your wrath has come, and the time of the dead, that they should be judged, and that you should reward your servants the prophets and the saints, and those who fear Your name, small and great, and should destroy those who destroy the earth." Then the temple of God was opened in heaven, and the ark of his covenant was seen in his temple. And there were lightnings, noises, thunderings, an earthquake, and great hail. (Rev. 11:15–19)

This passage holds great significance in relation to the rapture. That the seventh trumpet announces the Kingdom of God in fullness and judgment is a clear indication that the mighty appearing of Yeshua is being announced. Indeed, this is the time of his wrath and the establishment of his reign. This takes place with the rapture of the saints even as the saints are rewarded (v. 18).[55]

The seventh trumpet brings this transitional age to its climax; seven again denotes perfection or completion.[56] The saved representatives of Israel, with the whole body of believers, worship God. Great power is seen at his throne. Again, the imagery before the throne of God with the ark in the heavenly Temple finds its parallel in Exodus. Recall the awesome power of God in lightning, thunder, and earthquake on Mount Sinai after the Exodus when the Law was given. Indeed, the glory cloud rested upon the mountain; this cloud is the transitional plane between the dimensions of heaven and earth. Looking into the glory cloud, the throne of God can be seen. Therefore the manifestations in Revelation 11:19 and in Exodus 19 are similar.

A Vision of the 144,000 (Rev. 14:1–5)

With the sounding of the seventh trumpet, Yeshua appears on Mount Zion. With him are the previously mentioned 144,000 (see Chapter 3). In Revelation 14 the 144,000 are not explicitly revealed to be the saved remnant of Israel, but because the 144,000 are described as the saved remnant of Israel in Revelation 7, I believe it is best to see this group as such, the Jewish members of the body of the Messiah. They are "first

---

55. Bauckham has noted before that the last of each of the series of seven takes us to the ultimate climax because the seventh in the series of seals includes the trumpets and the final trumpet includes the seven bowls. So the end of each series takes us to the final climax (p. 40). Osborn sees the final consummation announced here, but the actual climax before the sixth bowl (p. 432).

56. Some Christians, and rabbis, believe that spiritual time totals 7,000 years: 2,000 years from Adam to Abraham, 2,000 from Abraham to Messiah's First Coming, 2,000 in this transitional age, and 1,000 years of the Millennial Sabbath Age.

fruits" (Rev. 14:4) because Jewish believers are the first fruits of the harvest out of all the nations. They reflect the state of all true believers. In other words, salvation is to come, as more will be harvested into the Kingdom of God, especially in the Age to Come. This is a picture of the Church.

Their virgin status denotes spiritual purity, not necessarily an unmarried state.[57]Again, their worship ascends and joins with the worship of those in heaven. How glorious that the blood of Yeshua and his sanctifying power can cause human beings to be described as "without fault." The Father's name is on their foreheads. The People of God are marked and will not go through the bowls of God's wrath unlike those with the mark of the beast (Rev. 14:9).

Proclamations by Three Angels (Rev. 14:6–13)

The pictures in this section prepare the body of believers for the rapture. With the blowing of the seventh trumpet, the first angel proclaims that it is now time to choose the everlasting gospel or suffer the wrath of God. A second angel announces Babylon's fall as part of the judgment of the wrath of God on the kingdoms of this world. (This fall is more vividly described in Revelation 17–18 and Chapter 4 of this book.) The last angel warns not to partake of the mark of the beast in or you will suffer the wrath of God, torment with fire and brimstone before God's holy angels. I do not believe this speaks of everlasting damnation, but rather of the experience of the bowls of God's judgments in Revelation 16. Of course, those who ultimately refuse the offer of redemption

---

57. Bauckham cites that virginity is symbolic for purity because an army of males must have ritual purity to go forth to war (p. 78). Both Osborn and Bauckham disagree with me and see the 144,000 as the ascended Church. For Bauckham, they are martyred.

experience a final separation from God *and* the wrath of His everlasting judgment. That the smoke of their torment ascends forever speaks of the judgment's permanence for those who refuse God's redemption even when the bowls of His wrath are poured out (Rev. 14:10–11). God's wrath on earth foreshadows the judgment of hell and the lake of fire.

Then two greatly comforting words are given which apply to all saints who suffer persecution for the Lord. First, the saints are told to be the patient and firm in their faith because they know God will ultimately bring full and fair judgment. Second, if they die for the Lord, they know that they will soon be with him in resurrection bodies. Their works of faith will follow them as eternal rewards. The fruit harvested during their lives will be an eternal crown of glory.

The Exodus Rapture: Into the Glory Cloud (Rev. 14:14–16)

Finally, the moment has come; the rapture is about to take place. As described in Matthew 24 and parallel synoptic passages, the Lord returns to gather his harvest from all over the earth:

> Then the sign of the Son of Man will appear in heaven, and then all of the tribes of the earth will mourn, and they will see the Son of Man coming on the clouds of heaven with power and great glory. And he will send his angels with a great sound of a trumpet, and they will gather together his elect from the four winds, from one end of heaven to the other. (Matt. 24:30–31)

In a sense, the rapture of the saints parallels the gathering of the children of Israel who are scattered back to their Land:

> So it shall be in that day. That the great trumpet will be blown; they will come, who are about to perish in the land of Assyria, and they who are outcasts in the land of Egypt, and shall worship the Lord in the holy mount at Jerusalem. (Isa. 27:13)

These pictures surely foreshadow the wonderful description found in Revelation:

> And I looked, and behold, a white cloud, and on the cloud sat One like the Son of Man, having on his head a golden crown, and in his hand a sharp sickle. And another angel came out of the temple, crying with a loud voice to him who sat on the cloud, "Thrust in your sickle and reap, for the time has come for you to reap, for the harvest of the earth is ripe." So he who sat on the cloud thrust in his sickle on the earth, and the earth was reaped.[58] (Rev. 14:14–15)

---

58.   Osborn and Bauckham both agree that this is the harvest into salvation and is the consummation at the end of the age (Osborn p. 550–557; Bauckham p. 95). They argue against the view that the two harvests in this section, of grain and grapes, are both harvests for judgment and wrath, which is the view of some commentators. Bauckham gives an extended argument that the harvest of grain is not ever connected to the wrath of God. He sees the harvest as twofold, the covenanted nations into salvation and the final judgment of the unconverted nations. He notes that any Jew would have seen the 144,000 as first fruits leading to the fuller harvest to follow in Revelation 14. This comes close to admitting that the 144,000 are Jews, which Bauckham does not embrace. Again, he notes that first fruits is a pledge and Revelation 14:4 is connected to Revelation 14:14–16. These images correspond to the gathering of the nations to Armageddon and the judgment of the nations at the Parousia (Rev. 16:12–14, 19:15).

Yeshua reaps the grain harvest, gathering the believers up into heaven with him. Note the golden crown on the head of Yeshua.[59] The victory in the rapture of the saints assures the downfall of Satan, the beast, and the kingdoms of this world. The Church is raised into glory to come with him as his armies. The Bride of the Messiah returns to rule with him and to establish his Kingdom in all the earth! Believers will have escaped the forces of the anti-Messiah in a mighty Exodus through the glory cloud to the other side. Those who were martyred are also now seen as victorious.

The escape of the believers is more extraordinary than the Israelite's escape through the sea because Revelation brings a finality of judgment that was only proximate in Exodus.[60] Israel experienced protection from the plagues in Egypt and observed the drowning of the Egyptians from the other side of the sea. In the same way, the true disciples of Yeshua will experience deliverance from the plagues of the seven seals and seven trumpets in their natural bodies but will execute with Yeshua God's judgments of the seven bowls in the Second Coming. With his People protected, prepared, and plied for vindication, God's wrath is now able to be unleashed in awesome fury.

---

59. Bauckham strongly supports this interpretation (p. 95). This is a common view among interpreters. However, there are some interpreters that do think the figure is not Yeshua but an angel.

60. "The plagues of the seven trumpets (Rev. 8:6–9:21) and the seven bowls (Rev. 16:1–21), ... form a highly schematized literary pattern which itself conveys meaning. Their content suggests, among many other things, the plagues of Egypt which accompanied the Exodus" (Bauckham, p. 20). On the theme of this last great deliverance after the plagues and war parallel to the Exodus from the sea, see Bauckham p. 70. The wealth of parallelism in Bauckham is a wonderful support to this book. Osborn also notes the parallel of deliverance through the sea and the deliverance of God's People in the Last Days (p. 562).

CHAPTER SIX

The Wrath of the Lamb and His Armies

The theme of the wrath of the Lamb is found in Revelation 14:17–20, 15–16, and 18:20–19.

Every moment of history has led up to this point in the heavenly battle of God versus Satan. With the army of saints by his side, Yeshua leads the charge to once and for all reconcile man to God. Judgment is swift, and those whose hearts have been hardened will drown in its wake, just like the Egyptians, who so doggedly pursued Israel and were drowned in the Red Sea.

The Harvest of the Wicked (Rev. 14:17–20)

In verses immediately following the description of the rapture, an angel with a sharp sickle comes from the Temple of God in heaven. This angel also gathers a harvest of "... the clusters of the vine of the earth, for her grapes are fully ripe." The vine of the earth is gathered and thrown into the winepress of the wrath of God. As grapes represent blood in sacrificial ceremony, so the wrath of God squeezes out the blood, or the life, of those who experience it. The quantity of blood outside the city reaches to the horses' bridles.[61]

This particular passage is an introduction to what follows. *With the rapture of the saints, God's wrath can be poured out upon the world. The believers will join Yeshua to execute judgment upon the armies that have come up to Jerusalem.* A worldwide judgment produces much death. The description of the amount of blood is metaphorical, as though the blood were to be gathered in one locality, but the winepress of wrath covers the earth.

The dimensions of this wrath are described in different pictures. First are the seven bowls of God's wrath, which give a picture of plagues and other types of judgments poured out on all the earth.[62] There are two other pictures that, I believe, will be fulfilled simultaneously with this: the final fall of Babylon and the destruction of the armies of the anti-Messiah, whose forces include soldiers from all nations. *Just as Pharaoh's armies were drowned in the Red Sea in God's wrath, so the anti-Messiah is drowned in the judgments of God, poured out at the return of Yeshua with his victorious armies.*

The Seven Bowls of God's Wrath (Revelation 15–16)

In Revelation 15 the seven angels with the seven last plagues come out of the heavenly Temple to complete the wrath of God. Verse 2 also foreshadows the victory of the saints: John

---

61. Bauckham is very clear on the grape harvest being a harvest into wrath (p. 95). His argument for two different harvests is persuasive.

62. The bowls of God's wrath are again seen as parallel to the Exodus plagues in Bauckham (p. 96–98). Osborn essentially notes the song of Moses and the Lamb here as an Exodus motif, and the bowls again echo the Egyptian plagues (p. 550). Keener says, "By recalling the plagues, this series of judgments also reminds believers that as God protected his own people in Goshen during the plagues, so he will protect them in his judgments" (p. 393).

sees a sea of glass mingled with fire upon which stand the saints who have the victory over the beast, his image, and his mark. They have the harps of God. Is this a picture of the saints after the rapture? They will be ordered into ranks to soon return with the Lord. It is of the nature of apocalyptic literature to repeat and make allusion to earlier covered themes and also later themes. There is overlap. The rapture is anticipated in the announcement in Revelation 11, described in Revelation 14, and then perhaps the results are shown in this picture. At any rate, according to the plan of the book, the saints do not remain in heaven but are destined very soon to return to earth to rule and reign with the Messiah.

In verses 3–4, the saints sing the song of Moses and the Lamb. There is no false separation between the revelation of Moses and the revelation of Yeshua. They are one and lead to the ultimate fulfillment of the prophetic hope that "… all nations shall come and worship before you, for your judgments have been manifested" (v. 4b). These short verses illustrate God's rescuing of his People in the rapture (the martyrs mentioned in Revelation 5 and the raptured saints mentioned in Revelation 14) and his great wrath for those who reject him. The verses connect the Exodus, where God's People watch unscathed as pharaoh's army is engulfed by the waves of the Red Sea, to the vision that includes the victory of martyrs over the beast and might also include those who were resurrected and translated into glory.[63]

---

63. Commentators who see the Exodus typology as a key in these passages make a great deal of these verses. Stern notes the parallel to the post-Exodus song (p. 832). Beasley-Murray says that this verse compares the last deliverance with the Exodus (p. 1298). "By noting Moses and the Lamb together, we have a connecting of the great deliverances but the greater one is the last (Is. 51:9–11)." Bauckham suggests that John may have connected Isaiah 53 language of the suffering servant with the martyrs here (p. 71, 98). He then goes on to say, "In 15:2–4, the Christian martyrs, victorious in heaven,

After the song, John sees the Temple filled with the power of God's glory. No one may enter it until the plagues are complete. Here is another parallel to later in Exodus, wherein the glory of God filled the Tabernacle blocking the priests from ministering.

After this glory is revealed, the charge is given to pour out the bowls of the wrath of God. The wrath of God parallels both the plagues of Egypt[64] and the drowning of Pharaoh's troops in the sea. However, the exact nature of the plagues' progression is different because in this case, I believe, the saints are not on earth.

God's Wrath Poured out

The *first bowl* issues in foul and loathsome sores upon those who had the mark of the beast. This directly parallels the sixth plague of Egypt (Ex. 9:8–11).

With the *second bowl,* the sea becomes blood and the living creatures in the sea die. The *third bowl* also turns water to blood, in this case rivers and springs of water. Because the wicked have shed the blood of saints, their penalty is to drink blood. Whether this is literal or is symbolic of putrid red waters, the penalty is fitting and directly correlates to the first plague of Egypt (Ex. 7:14–24).

---

are seen as the people of the new Exodus, standing beside a heavenly Red Sea, through which they have passed and singing a version of the song of praise to God, which Moses and the People of Israel sang after their deliverance form Pharaoh at the Red Sea (Ex. 15). Moreover, the plagues, which are God's judgment on their enemies in this context (Rev. 15:1, 5, 16–21), are modeled on the plagues of Egypt at the time of the Exodus." Osborn also states, "Like Moses after the victory, they sing a song" (p. 563). Bauckham sees universal hope for the conversion of the nations in this verse as well, "the Exodus deliverance brings the nations to God" (p. 101).

64. As seen by most commentators, Stern and Beasley-Murray note the boils as parallel to Egypt (Stern, p. 833; Beasley-Murray, p. 1299).

The *fourth bowl* brings scorching heat from the sun.[65] Men are so deeply deceived and steeped in sin that they blaspheme the Name of God instead of repenting.

How could this be possible? Surely the Devil knows his time is short. Could mankind be deceived into cursing God as the solution? Perhaps Satan convinces the world that good is evil and evil is good, leading men to curse God as a false god, that he might be empowered to bring deliverance. Of course, Satan will not be able to remove these plagues any more than Pharaoh's magicians could remove the plagues of their day.

A picture of this period is found in Isaiah 26:28–27:1. God calls his People into their chambers to hide themselves until the indignation is past. The Lord "comes out of his place to punish the inhabitants of the earth for their iniquity." The Lord, with his "severe sword... will punish Leviathan, the fleeing serpent."

In Isaiah 60:2–3 the period of the Second Coming is described in these terms:

> For behold, the darkness shall cover the earth, and deep darkness the people; but the Lord will arise over you, and his glory will be seen upon you. The Gentiles shall come to your light, and kings to the brightness of your rising.

The fifth bowl brings darkness over the earth. This corresponds to the next-to-last plague in Exodus, which led Pharaoh to consider allowing the Israelites to leave before his

---

65. A major change in weather patterns could easily cause this. If other calamities disrupt electric power, men could be faced with a situation with no possibility of relief.

heart was hardened and he refused. In Revelation the people's great pain causes them to blaspheme God again.[66]

With *the sixth bowl,* the river Euphrates dries up. This prepares the way for armies to come from the east. Paralleling the second plague on Egypt, unclean spirits like frogs are seen coming out of the mouths of the dragon, the beast, and the false prophet. These demonic spirits do signs and wonders. I believe they must do their false signs through wicked rulers who are yielded to them. Deceived people who are influenced by these spirits will follow these wicked rulers. There is such deep deception that the false rulers of this world believe the Devil is the one to be followed and that Satan can win against the Messiah and his armies—just as Pharaoh's troops followed the Israelites into the sea under the deception that they could defeat the People of God!

Once the believers in Yeshua have been taken in the rapture, only Israel will be an impediment to their schemes. I believe the world will see Israel as the source of the problem and will falsely believe that if they destroy her, the plagues will cease and the supernatural power of the dragon will restore order. So the armies of nations gather to the place called Armageddon. The world will see the battle in terms of

---

66. The plagues are sure marks that the human race is under judgment and in need of redemption. Such plagues are suffered corporately by humanity, not always as a result of individual sin and judgment. All such judgments should lead mankind to repent and to seek the mercy of God. It is a result of sowing and reaping. Yet the response of much of humanity is to debate the problem of evil: How can God be good and allow such human suffering? How blind the race of man is! Rather the conclusion should be that man must be exceedingly wicked if God, who is good, allows such suffering and pain. If we could see in the light of God's righteousness, we would find that the level of human suffering could have been much worse, but God has been exceedingly merciful and patient, waiting for humankind to return to him.

supernatural power against supernatural power.[67] However, they will be allied with the wrong power. This is an incredibly supernatural period of time.

The seventh bowl is the bowl of perfect completion. It is announced with the words, "It is done." There are thunderings, lightnings, and a mighty earthquake (see Zechariah 14). The great city is divided into three parts and the cities of the nations fall in earthquakes. The great city could be the center of the Babylonian system most closely represented by Rome in the first century. It could also be Jerusalem, not yet submitted to Yeshua. (We know from Zechariah 14 that a great earthquake will divide Jerusalem in the days of the last battle.) No matter the identity of the city, the Babylonian system receives the full wrath of God. So great is the judgment that it is thus described in apocalyptic symbolism: "Every island fled away, and the mountains were not found. And great hail from Heaven fell upon men... " (Vv. 20–21a). In spite of all this, men blasphemed God.

Only the final defeat of all the armies of the anti-Messiah will break the delusion. This is the theme of Revelation 19.

Timing of the Seven Bowls

Before turning to Revelation 19 and its picture of victory, I think it is important to discuss the time frame of the seven bowls. I believe the seven bowls happen in a very brief period of time. This period is symbolized in the Jewish calendar as the ten-day period between the Feast of the Trumpets

---

67. It is easy to see the potential of a world body such as the United Nations in a unified military thrust. With the New Age religious orientation, the world will look at Evangelicals and Jews as the two most narrow-minded peoples on the earth and as a roadblock to a world religion of maturity and the mutual affirmation of various pantheistic and polytheistic traditions. The weak relativistic governments yield to the violent power of Islam. Even now such a lineup is seen in the world situation.

(Rosh Hashanah) and the holy day of Yom Kippur (Day of Atonement). It is possible that the period of the outpouring of the wrath of God is literally that short. However, the ten-day period of the calendar may be more symbolic of this last brief, but most intense, period of judgment. These key holy days hold important significance in Jewish spiritual rituals.

I should note that although Passover/Exodus provides our primary interpretive framework, Rosh Hashanah, or the Feast of Trumpets, seems a natural connection to the book of Revelation from the blowing of the seven shofars (as we have previously stated). The blowing of the seventh of these trumpets unleashes the bowls of God wrath. In Jewish tradition Rosh Hashanah announces God's judgments. The days between Rosh Hashanah and Yom Kippur, the Day of Atonement, is a period known as the Days of Awe. These days are days of judgment and even vengeance for the unrepentant, in Jewish tradition. They are days of mercy for the repentant. They continue until Yom Kippur when the repentant may be forgiven and have their names written in the Book of Life. Therefore, I think it is quite reasonable to see the bowls of wrath in this context.

The Announcement of the Marriage Supper of the Lamb (Rev. 19:1–10)

Chapter 19 begins with another picture of a great multitude in heaven praising God and saying, "Salvation and glory and honor and power to the Lord our God!" He is praised for judging the great harlot and avenging the blood of his servants. The twenty-four elders again bow down and worship God. All are called upon to praise God.

In verses 7–9 there is an announcement of the marriage of the Lamb, whose wife has made herself ready. "And to her it was granted to be arrayed in fine linen, clean and bright, for *the fine linen is the righteous acts of the saints...* Blessed are those who are called to the marriage supper of the Lamb— These are the true sayings of God" (vs. 8–9, emphasis mine). The symbolic meaning of the white garments and perhaps of all priestly garments from ancient times is to be clothed in righteousness.

This marriage is celebrated with a huge feast that all of the nations will attend. I believe this marriage supper is the worldwide coronation ceremony of the King and his Bride, the body of believers. The Church is to be the ruling Queen, standing at his side in the Age to Come.

When Does the Marriage Supper Take Place?

Many have speculated concerning the timing of the marriage supper. Some have seen it as occurring in the first days after the rapture or while the saints are in heaven during the seven years of tribulation.[68] I disagree with both of these views. As mentioned above I believe the judgments of seven bowls takes place between Rosh Hashanah on Tishri 1 and Yom Kippur on Tishri 10, leading to the repentance of all the nations. Five days later, on Tishri 15, comes *Sukkot* (Feast of Tabernacle), an eight-day celebration that is the greatest festival on ancient Israel's calendar. *I believe the marriage supper is part of the*

---

68. Clearly the wedding of the Lamb takes place after the judgments of the Last Days, contrary to many dispensational teachers who strangely place the rapture at the beginning of a seven-year tribulation and then the marriage supper during the tribulation. My interpretation places it during the first Feast of Tabernacles after the Second Coming.

celebration of Sukkot because of the symbolism of the fall feasts. This would align with the prophecy given in Zechariah 14 in that all nations send representatives to celebrate this feast in Israel. This feast would then be the annual anniversary celebration of the establishment of the rule of the Messiah and his Bride upon the earth. It would also be the annual memorial of the great wedding.

The Return of Yeshua with His Saints (Rev. 19:11–16)

In one of the most powerful passages in Scripture, John describes a vision of heaven open. He sees One riding upon a white horse with the armies of heaven, clothed in fine white and clean linen, following him. He is called "Faithful and True. In righteousness he judges and makes war." The description of Yeshua continues:

> His eyes were like a flame of fire, and on his head were many crowns. He had a name written that no one knew except himself. He was clothed with a robe dipped in blood, and his name is called The Word of God... Out of his mouth goes a sharp sword, that with it he should strike the nations. And he himself will rule them with a rod of iron. He Himself treads the winepress of the fierceness and wrath of Almighty God. And he has on his robe and on his thigh a name written, KING OF KINGS AND LORD OF LORDS. (Rev. 19:12–13, 15–16)

This picture is also found in Isaiah, where it says the Messiah will strike the earth with the rod from his mouth and with the breath of his lips he will slay the wicked (Isa. 11:4).

The Defeat of the Anti-Messiah and His Forces (Rev. 19:17–21)

With Yeshua descending from heaven, the final battle of Armageddon or the battle of Jerusalem begins. I believe Satan himself will be directly involved in this battle and will perhaps even be visible in this final conflagration. His appearing as an angel of light according to other biblical texts could be part of the world's reason for following him. The Revelation text says that the dragon draws the nations into this battle. He is seen as the ultimate false god. With this battle, I believe the veil will be lifted between the seen and the unseen worlds. People will see angelic and demonic hosts at war, Israel battling the earthly armies of the beast (Zech. 12:1–9), and resurrected saints in supernatural bodies coming with the Lord to aid in the attack.

During the battle, an angel invites the birds to come to the feast of judgment. This is paralleled in Luke 17, "Wherever the body is, there the eagles will be gathered together" (v. 37). The birds of prey are told they will eat the flesh of all kinds of people—kings, captains, warriors, commoners and slaves—and horses.

It seems incredible that the forces of the beast, the anti-Messiah, would face the awesome supernatural armies of God. (But didn't Pharaoh pursue Israel into the sea despite the mighty signs and wonders that accompanied God's People?) What utter deception! Does the Devil even deceive himself, believing he can win? I believe so.

That deception has devastating consequences. A more complete description of this battle is found in Zechariah 14. The human armies of the anti-Messiah who are invading Israel are described as coming under a plague where their flesh melts on their bodies and their eyes dissolve in their sockets. They are utterly routed, just as the armies of Pharaoh were obliterated by the Red Sea's waves. The defeat of the anti-Messiah's forces rips away the veil of blindness over the nations. In the last invasion of Israel, this defeat is finalized.

> And in this mountain the Lord of hosts will make for all people a feast of choice pieces... And he will destroy on this mountain the surface of the covering cast over all people, and the veil that is spread over all nations. (Isa. 25:6–7)

The beast and false prophet, who did the signs and wonders, are captured. They are cast into the lake of fire, which burns with brimstone. The rest of the armies are killed with the sword from Christ's mouth. There is no contest. The Messiah with his victorious saints prevails!

Satan Is Bound for a Thousand Years (Rev. 20:1–3)

Of course, with the fall of Babylon and the defeat of the anti-Messiah and the false prophet, total victory must include the conquering of Satan, the dragon. He empowered and inspired the beast. In Revelation 20, an angel from heaven holds a key to the bottomless pit and a great chain. He is given the power to lay hold of the dragon and to bind him for 1,000 years in the bottomless pit. Satan is shut up with a seal on him, and he will no longer be able to deceive the nations.

The great encouragement to the body of believers is that *ultimate victory is assured.* Evil forces have been defeated; the marriage supper of the Lamb will occur; and the full establishment of the Kingdom of God has come. Welcome to the eternal Promised Land!

CHAPTER SEVEN

Entry into the Promised Land!

*The theme of the Promised Land is found
in Revelation 20:4–15 and 21–22.*

The end of Revelation shows the body of believers entering the Age to Come and reveals the conditions of that age. The parallels between the events of the Exodus and the End Times are very strong. In Exodus, after Israel received the Law, they were to defeat the enemies of God and take possession of the Promised Land, ushering in a type of the Age to Come. These epic battles are comparable to engagements of the Last Days before believers entered the ultimate Promised Land. Had Moses and the Israelites not sinned, Moses himself would have led the Israelites into the Promised Land, but due to Moses' disobedience, Joshua (the same name as Yeshua!) became the leader of the "entering in." Due to the unbelief of the Israelites, the crossing over took place forty years later than expected.

The Millennial Age and the Last Rebellion(Rev. 20:4–10)

Great controversy rages concerning the meaning of Revelation 20:4–10. A literal reading of this passage indicates a resurrection of the dead, initiating a 1,000-year period of peace under the Messiah's rule. The dead mentioned in this passage are only those who had been beheaded for their witness to Yeshua and who did not worship the beast or receive his mark. This is the first resurrection. Over these, death has no power, but they are called priests with God and reign with the Messiah.

However, most interpreters believe the resurrection mentioned here is not limited to the Last Days' martyrs even though this is what John saw. This is because 1 Corinthians 15 and 1 Thessalonians 4:16–17 indicate a resurrection of *all* of the saved at Yeshua's return. (In every age there is an opportunity for people to give themselves to the world, the flesh, and the Devil. Only those who do not do so are resurrected.)

After this 1,000-year period Satan escapes to deceive the nations again. A vast multitude, as numerous as the sand of the sea, goes up to the saints' camp and the beloved city.[69] However, a fire comes forth from God and devours them. The Devil is cast into the lake of fire, which leads to the great white throne judgment (Rev. 20:11–15).

The Amillennial Interpretation

The amillennial interpretation of this passage has held sway throughout most of Church history. It views Revelation 20:1–10 as simply recounting the content of the early chapters in a different way.[70] The first resurrection is viewed as the experience of being born again. Those who were born again

---

69. Could this be Jerusalem? The idea that a new generation has grown up and the God gives them a test at the end of the Millennial Age is fitting. The camp idea also fits the Exodus where the saints are in a camp with the presence of God. Jerusalem is described as the center of God's Kingdom and the place of his dwelling, so this would seem to fit best.

70. Augustine, in the fifth century, was a great proponent of this viewpoint. Basically, it was thought that the end of Roman opposition to the Church produced a situation in which Satan was bound. This binding was thought to be the condition of most of this age.

and died are alive in heaven and are reigning in heaven with the Messiah. The fullness of receiving their permanent resurrected bodies, however, was thought to await the Lord's return at the end of the 1,000 years. Ultimately, all of the saved and lost would be judged at one time at the end of the 1,000-year period, which was symbolic of the time frame between the First and Second Comings of Yeshua. The number 1,000 is 10 x 10 x 10, which is God's complete order for this age. The end of this age manifests the great rebellion against God and his People. This is seen as the same rebellion as is described throughout the book. The rebellion's defeat is seen depicted in Revelation 19. After this come Yeshua's return, the final judgment, and the new heaven and earth. No literal earthly Millennial Age is expected in the future; hence, the name *amillennial* or *present millennial*, to describe this view.

The Amillennialists points out how foolish it seems to believe in an age in which earthly nations continue while the resurrected rule and live side by side with the non-resurrected. For him, the passages in the Hebrew Scriptures concerning a worldwide commonwealth with Israel at the helm and Jerusalem as the capital are wooden literalism. He believes that the picture in the Prophets of a glorious age on earth with humankind living in prosperity, propagating children, and dying at ripe old ages is symbolic. The blessings of Israel in the classical amillennial scheme are interpreted as referring to the Church.

Critics of this view note that nothing in the Hebrew Scriptures indicates that these passages are symbolic. They show that the ancients understood the difference between a long life ending in death and eternal life (e.g., the meaning of the tree of life giving everlasting life in the Garden of Eden). That distinction was appreciated. Also, they reject the application of blessing to the Church instead of Israel because there is nothing in the Hebrew text to indicate that this is so.

Some Amillennialists today are stressing the continuity of the new earth with the present earth and even have a place for the Jewish people to have a special inheritance in their own land in this everlasting age.[71]

Premillennial Interpretation

The *premillennial view*, which I hold, believes that there are two stages to the Age to Come. The first stage is the Millennial Age, which is established after Yeshua's return. The second stage is the coming of the new heaven and earth, which takes place after the great white throne judgment.[72]

What Is the Nature of the Millennial Age? Although the Millennial Age is a glorious age of peace and prosperity in which all nations are unified under the Messiah's rule, it is not in a state of perfection. Even the Prophets' glorious description tells of an age in which death still ultimately claims the lives of earthly humankind. However, the human race lives to great old age. It is therefore a transitional age of a higher order than the present transitional age.

The Millennial Age is such a glorious age of the Spirit that

---

71. This was the view of Dr. Richard Lovelace, of Gordon Conwell Theological Seminary. He personally conveyed this in conversation. Since that time I have met others with a similar view.

72. For a presentation supporting this view see Stern p. 842. Stern also includes references from Jewish sources for the Millennial Age. Bauckham states, "The goal of the new Exodus is still to be attained, when Christ's people will reign with him as priests on earth (20:4–6, 22:3–5) attaining their theocratic independence in the Promised Land" (p. 72). This does not mean that Bauckham ultimately supports a literal Millennial Age, but he does not support the view that this is just symbolic of the Church Age.

I believe it to be an age of promise paralleling Israel's entering into the Promised Land. All nations will celebrate the biblical feasts unto Yeshua, the knowledge of the Lord will cover the earth as the water covers the beds of the seas, and all flesh will know the reality of the Spirit in the first part of that age (Joel 2:28; Isa. 45:22–25; Zech. 14:9; Isa. 65:20–25;66:23). In this age all the promises to regather the Jewish people and to make Israel a praise of the whole earth will be fulfilled.

Why Is There a Millennial Age Before Entering the Promised Land? The Millennial Age serves several purposes. First, I believe God works through a restoration process whereby the effects of the Fall are reversed, somewhat like a movie running backward. The Millennium is the restoration of pre-Flood longevity. During the pre-Flood period, man lived for more than 900 years. In the Millennium, Isaiah says that one who dies at 100 years will be considered to be under a curse (Isa. 65:20). In reversing the curse, longevity is recovered.

Second, with Satan bound, I believe man will be able to fully live out the principles of faith, healing, and prosperity promised in the Law. This will be a worldwide condition. All God's Laws (principles) and promises will be found to be fully effective in an earthly state. Of course, human ability will be the result of faith and the power of the Spirit. I believe God wants to demonstrate his truth in a special way during this age. This will be remembered throughout eternal ages.

How Do We Interpret the First and Second Resurrections in Revelation 20? The first resurrection is the resurrection of the saints who are the ruling alongside Yeshua as his

Queen. I see nothing ludicrous in the resurrected ruling the non-resurrected. The interchange between two types of humans on earth is no stranger than the interchange between humans and angels or between the resurrected Messiah and his disciples during the forty days between his Resurrection and his Ascension. Indeed, this forty-day period may have been a foreshadowing of the Millennial Age. Those in the first resurrection have overcome; the second death—the everlasting separation from God in the lake of fire that takes place after the final judgment—has no power over them.[73] The second resurrection refers to the judgment at the great white throne described as taking place after the Millennium in Revelation 20 as described below.

How Can Rebellion Occur If Yeshua Is Ruling? In Revelation 20:7–9 the last great rebellion begins. I do not believe Yeshua and the resurrected saints will always be localized in specific places on earth as they rule. I believe Yeshua will certainly and regularly appear to be on the throne and ruling in Jerusalem, but I also believe that Yeshua and the saints will have access to heaven and earth. As the Millennial Age continues, the rule with a rod of iron of the Messiah and his saints will become less dominant. More rule and authority will transfer to humans who are still in their earthly bodies. This is similar to the situation in which the Israelites rebelled against Moses when he was absent in the heights of Mt. Sinai.

Remember, too, by the end of the Millennium, all those who survived to enter this age will have passed away and God

---

73. For support of this inclusive view, see Stern p. 845 and also, Beasley-Murray who states, "The reign has to include all who overcome and thus the whole Church" (p. 1306).

has to test the generations born during the latter part of this age. The unbinding of Satan's implies that the power of deception will be unleashed, creating a situation to test the hearts of the nations. It will look as though God's designated rulers are in the wrong and are to be overthrown.

This rebellion produces no drawn-out period as in the tribulation of the Last Days. Once the hearts are tested, the judgment is swift. The Devil is judged and sent to his eternal doom.

The Great White Throne Judgment (Rev. 20:11–15)

The great white throne provides an image of God's final judgment before the new heaven and earth. All of the dead who have not been resurrected will be alive at this time. This judgment is for the lost from all ages before the Millennial Age and for the saved and lost that died during the age. I believe it is a clear implication of Revelation 20:12 that some of those who appear before the throne of God are saved; their names are found in the Book of Life. The section is beyond literal human understanding because it says that death and *Hades* were cast into the lake of fire. This simply means that death and *Hades* are finally and forever destroyed from the society of the redeemed.

Those whose names are not found in the Book of Life are cast into the lake of fire. That lake seems to be a place of turmoil and despair (suffering the full consequences of human self-centeredness and separation from God).

The New Heaven and Earth (Rev. 21:1–8)

There is some debate as to whether the new heaven and earth are a total renewal of this creation or a completely new creation. Either way, the reality of a universe that is fully freed from the bondage of corruption and decay is truly magnificent.[74]

John also sees a New Jerusalem coming down from heaven as a bride adorned for her husband (v. 2). Is the New Jerusalem the People of God or the dwelling place of the People of God? I believe it is both. God now includes the saved from all ages within the Bride of Messiah. The great promise of the Prophets is now fulfilled—God abides with his People forever:

> Behold, the tabernacle of God is with men, and he will dwell with them, and they shall be his people, and God himself will be with them and be their God. And God will wipe away every tear from their eyes; there shall be no more death, nor sorrow, nor crying,and there shall be no more pain, for the former things have passed away. (Rev. 21:3–4)

What words can possibly be added to this glorious expression? The Beginning and the End, the Alpha and the Omega, makes all things new. He gives the water of life freely to all who will drink of it. Those who overcome will be children of God forever. He will dwell with us and in us as his own Tabernacle. However, verse 6 says all the wicked will be excluded.

---

74. On this subject, the words of Metzger are pertinent: "Whether John would have us think of the new heavens and new earth as a transformation of the existing order, or whether this present cosmos will come to an end and a new creation will replace it, it is not quite clear. In any case, the word *new* used by John does not mean simply another, but a new kind of heaven and earth" (p. 98).

The New Jerusalem (Rev. 21:9–21)

A wonderful account is given in this passage of the New Jerusalem descending. Read the passage and allow the grandeur of the description to sink in. It is difficult to tell where to draw the line between the literal and the symbolic. This passage strains at realities that are difficult for man to comprehend.

The New Jerusalem is both the People and the center of the order of God in the Age to Come. God dwells in the midst of his People, hence, in the midst of the New Jerusalem. The body of believers and the city are the Temple of God in the Age to Come.[75]

The walls of the city are great and high with twelve gates. Angels are over each gate, giving a picture of majesty. Each gate has upon it the names of the twelve tribes of Israel. In the Torah, God said his Name would forever be "The God of Abraham, Isaac, and Jacob." Faith is rooted in Israel, and from Jewish people this faith was spread to the world. God will yet fully recover the meaning of Israel and restore this nation to the one olive tree of God (Rom. 11:24–29). God will redeem all that is truly good. It is indeed significant, therefore, that God forever will identify the New Jerusalem with the Israelite roots of redemptive history.

Out of Israel came the twelve apostles. Hence, the foundations of the walls have upon them the names of the apostles. The faith is thus represented by its great historic

---

75. Bauckham says, "The New Jerusalem is a place of security and provision in all ways... the place where heaven and earth meet at the center of the earth from which God rules his land and the nations and to which the nations are drawn for enlightenment" (p. 132). Osborn also argues that the New Jerusalem is both the place and the People (p. 733).

foundations in the apostles, but also stretches back beyond this to the twelve patriarchs.[76]

The city is like a huge cube with its width and its length given as 12,000 furlongs.[77] This is 1,380 miles! The walls' measurement of 144 cubits is a multiple of 12. The dimensions are again symbolic, twelve being the number of Israel and the People of God.

Gold is the royal metal, the predominant material in the New Jerusalem. There are also many varieties of precious stones. Each of the twelve foundations has its own precious gem decor. The twelve gates are made of pearl.

Beyond all these majestic descriptions is the fact that the glory of God illuminates the city, and he dwells in it. The Lamb as well is its light. The gates are forever open; all of the saved walk in this light forever. The kings of all the nations, who are part of the new heavens and earth, bring their glory into it. The glory and honor of the nations is also brought into it. No corruption shall ever defile it.

It is important to state that this passage presents the Kingdom in such a way that ethnic identities are preserved. Each nation has its own contribution to bring. This means not only gold and silver, but also distinctive cultural contributions. The God who loved variety in creation in Genesis 1 still loves variety in the human community. There is room for an optimistic hope for the redemption of nations or ethnic peoples.[78]

---

76. Osborn supports this interpretation and sees "Israel and the Church on the gates and foundation stones" (p. 752).

77. Some question the cube idea and say that it could be a pyramid with the throne on the top.

78. Stern quotes George Ladd and notes that Isaiah 60 is the context for the nations coming to the light of God (p. 854). Then he continues, "In the divine consummation, the redeemed will consist of people from every nation and tribe and people and tongue

The River of Life: Paradise Restored (Rev. 22:1–5)

The river of the water of life, clear as crystal, comes forth from the throne of God. Indeed, the water of life is found in a believer drinking deeply of his/her relationship with God. This is life! On the banks of the river are twelve trees of life bearing twelve fruits. This is the food for the People of God. Whereas Adam and Eve were banned from paradise and the tree of life in the Garden of Eden, now mankind is restored to paradise. However, it is a better paradise than was ever lost. The leaves of the trees heal the nations. In other words, the life that comes from God will provide total and everlasting healing.

The curse is ended; the throne of God and the Lamb are in the midst of the City of God and his servants will serve and dwell with God. How wonderful are these words:

> They shall see his face, and his name shall be on their foreheads. And there shall be no night there. They need no lamp, nor light of the sun, for the Lord God gives them light. And they shall reign forever and ever. (Rev. 22:4–5)

(7:9) who will not lose their national identity. John's language means no more than the statements of the prophets, 'and many people shall come and say, "Come let us go up to the mountain of the Lord, to the house of the God of Jacob."' (Isaiah 2:3) This is the affirmation of the universality of the knowledge of God, as promised in Jeremiah's presentation of the New Covenant." Also Bauckham comments, "Humanity does make a contribution to the New Jerusalem. It consummates human history and culture to the extent they have been dedicated to God" (p. 135). Later he states, "The nations walk by its light. The kings of the earth bring their glory into it. The glory and honor of the nations are brought into it. The kings of the earth formerly opposed Yeshua and his people" (p. 138). He also sees the basis as Isaiah 60 and sees that after the wrath of God, the nations are ultimately converted.

Closing Exhortations and Warnings (Rev. 22:6–21)

The closing makes it clear that for the People of God, the end of this age is forever on the doorstep. It could all come about very quickly. The Lamb of God can say, *"Behold, I am coming quickly! Blessed is he who keeps the words of the prophecy of this book"* (Rev. 22:7).

How do believers "keep" the words of such a prophecy? They are kept by holy, fruitful Kingdom living. They are kept by understanding the forces of evil and conducting spiritual warfare with the certainty of ultimate victory. They rescue the lost and serve so that the body might be whole. They need to recognize the forces of the anti-Messiahs that are already in the world. They must resist the lure of Babylon, which is a spiritual reality in every period of this transitional age. "The time is near" (v. 10). A time of division is coming wherein the holy and the unholy, the just and the unjust, the righteous and the filthy will fully manifest the extremes of good and evil before the great day of Yeshua's return.

Yeshua Speaks

Yeshua explains that he will come quickly and bring his reward. He reminds believers that they will receive the lasting fruit of their lives and the separation that is coming will lead to the everlasting separation. Those who keep God's commandments have the right to the tree of life and access to the gates of the city. However, outside the Kingdom of God will dwell all the unrighteous *"dogs and sorcerers, and sexually immoral and murderers and idolaters, and whoever loves and practices a lie"* (v. 15).

Yeshua states his identity as not only the Angel of the Covenant in the Hebrew Scriptures, the divine Son of the Triune Godhead, but also as the Root and Offspring of David and as David's Son forever described as a human being. He is the Bright and Morning Star. The biblical teaching on the incarnation is that in Immanuel, "God with us," the Son forever remains human and divine. This is why Yeshua shows himself to have a real physical body after the Resurrection. The Book of Revelation should be interpreted in the light of the total witness of the New Covenant Scriptures.

The Call to Respond

The Spirit and the Bride of the Messiah recall that the water of life is not only available in the Age to Come. It is available now to those who will fully yield their lives to Yeshua's Lordship and the joy of walking with him. Hence, as in Isaiah 55 and John 7, there is an invitation to come and drink of the water of life freely.

However, John warns that the book of this prophecy is to be carefully preserved and not tampered with. Indeed, this is a warning to carefully handle the Word of God with great reverence concerning its intended meaning! The penalty for violating this is the loss of everlasting life in the Holy City of God.

Ours for the Taking

How amazing and wonderful! The Bible begins with paradise lost, but it ends with a greater paradise restored that can never again be lost. The Promised Land of the new heaven and earth is ours after all of the foreshadowing Exodus events and lands of promise are past. We have seen the Exodus from Egypt and into the Promised Land of ancient Israel; the exodus of the Pilgrims and the Puritans to the Promised Land of America, the great missionary base for the twentieth century; and the exodus of Jews from the nations back to their ancient Promised Land as part of God's preparation in the Last Days. We will yet see the exodus of God's People into the glory cloud, which will lead to the Promised Land of the Millennial Age.

All will end in that glorious Promised Land of the new heaven and earth with its New Jerusalem, where God will dwell in the midst of his People and wipe away every tear. We will live in joyful, loving community with God and his People forever! This is *the* sustaining hope in times of trial and the destiny of God's holy people:

> He who testifies to these things says, "Surely I am coming quickly." Amen. Even so, come, Lord Yeshua! The grace of our Lord Yeshua the Messiah be with you all. Amen. (Rev. 22:21)

References

Beasley-Murray, G. R. *The Revelation: New Bible Commentary,* Grand Rapids, Mich.: Eerdmans, 1970.

Bauckham, Richard. *The Theology of the Book of Revelation,* Cambridge: Cambridge University Press, 1993.

Gilmore, S. MacLean. *The Revelation of St. John, The Interpreter's One Volume Commentary on the Bible,* New York: Abington, 1971.

Keener, Craig. *Revelation: The NIV Application Commentary,* Grand Rapids, Mich.: Zondervan, 2000.

Metzger, Bruce M. *Breaking the Code, Understanding the Book of Revelation,* Nashville: Abington, 1993.

Osborn, Grant R. *Revelation,* Grand Rapids, Mich.: Baker, 2006.

Stern, David. *Jewish New Testament Commentary,* Clarksville, Md.: Jewish New Testament Publications, 1992.

Tenney, Merrill C. *Interpreting Revelation,* Peabody, Mass.: Hendrickson, 2001.

Numbers in Revelation

People's ability to make much of every number in the Bible is extraordinary. Most people who engage in a heavy emphasis on biblical numerology are simply unaware of how tenuous their seemingly coherent schemes are. This was made clear in 1988 when teachers claimed that Jesus was returning on Rosh Hashanah (in September) of that year according to their calculations. There are many possible interpretations of numbers, age/day schemes, weekday schemes, and others. The "1,290 days" is taken to mean 1,290 *years* in some historical views.

Having offered these cautions, however, there are some numbers that seem to have clear symbolic meaning while possibly being more literal in ultimate fulfillment. Bible scholars usually see the following numbers and multiples as having set meanings. Biblical and intertestamental usage in ancient Jewish writings confirm these meanings:

3: The number representing the Godhead, the triune God.

6: The number of man, who was created on the sixth day of Creation. It can refer to man's self-sufficiency without God.

7: The number of perfection. The world was created in seven days. Rest is commanded on the seventh day. There are seven branches to the light of the holy lampstand. There are seven trumpets in Revelation that imply a seven-year time span, one for each trumpet blast, from one feast to the next.

8: The day of resurrection. It symbolizes new beginnings.

10: The number of completion. It includes the ten plagues on Egypt, one-tenth referring to tithe, ten as the number representing the confederacy against God in the Last Days.

12: The number of the tribes of Israel, the people of God. Note also that there were twelve apostles; their names and the names of the twelve tribes are inscribed on the gates and foundation stones of the New Jerusalem.

24: Twice the number of the People of God. This possibly indicates Israel and the Church together, represented by the twenty-four elders in heaven.

70: The number of the nations from the table of the nations (Gen. 10) and the sacrifices for the nations during the Feast of Tabernacles in Numbers. Seventy is a multiple of perfection and completeness (7 x 10).

666: The false trinity of human power and exaltation (the number six three times); the anti-Messiah.

1,260: Days of judgment (approximately three and a half years). The number 1,260 represents half a measure of perfect judgment because of God's mercy in shortening the days (Rev. 11:3).

144,000: The number of the sealed. It is a multiple of twelves and tens, a complete number of God's sealed ones.

The Time Frame

Asher Intrater

There are two passages tucked away in Leviticus that have a surprising impact on our understanding of how the biblical feasts foreshadow End Times prophecy. The first passage is the following:

> "When you come into the land which I give to you, and reap its harvest, then you shall bring a sheaf of the first fruits of your harvest to the priest. He shall wave the sheaf before the Lord, to be accepted on your behalf; on the day after the Sabbath the priest shall wave it." (Leviticus 23:10b–11)

This describes the Feast of First Fruits, which takes place on the first day of the week (i.e., Sunday) after Passover. Yeshua was crucified on Passover, and it was on the first day of the week after Passover that Yeshua was raised from the dead. Yeshua is called the "first fruits from the dead"(1 Cor. 15:20, 23).The Resurrection fulfilled that feast, and the Feast of First Fruits prophesied the Resurrection of Yeshua. The Holy Spirit was poured out on the Feast of Pentecost (also called *Shavu'ot* or the Feast of Weeks). The events surrounding the Church's birth were predicted in the Old Testament feasts. The feasts and their prophetic fulfillment all came to pass in the same year.

The biblical feasts are arranged in two groups: spring and fall feasts. The spring feasts were fulfilled through Yeshua in the first century. The fall feasts are connected to the End Times prophecies and have not yet been fulfilled. If the biblical pattern holds true, the End Times prophecies will be fulfilled on the days the feasts foreshadow them. The Feast of Trumpets relates to the trumpets in the Book of Revelation. The Day of Atonement corresponds to repentance in Israel at the time of Armageddon (Zech. 12:10, ff). The Feast of Tabernacles relates to the inaugural celebration of the messianic Kingdom. Together, the fall feasts foreshadow the Second Coming of Yeshua.

The second pertinent passage from Leviticus is 25:8–10a.

> "And you shall count seven sabbaths of years for yourself, seven times seven years; and the time of the seven sabbaths of years shall be to you forty-nine years. Then you shall cause the trumpet of the Jubilee to sound on the tenth day of the seventh month; on the Day of Atonement you shall make the trumpet to sound throughout all your land. And you shall consecrate the fiftieth year, and proclaim liberty throughout the land to all its inhabitants. It shall be a Jubilee for you."

The Book of Revelation contains three series of judgments. The first series is made up of seven seals, the second series is seven trumpets, and the third is seven bowls. The seven seals are keeping a scroll closed. The seals must be opened to read the scroll, which contains the remaining prophecies for the End Times.

The seven seals are the seven preparatory stages leading to the End Times events recorded in the scroll. Each seal opened inches closer to the trumpets and bowls. If the seven seals lead up to the events recorded in the scroll, they can be seen as encompassing longer periods of time that span Church history. The history of the Church is encapsulated in the descriptions of the seven seals.

The seven trumpets represent seven Feasts of Trumpets. The blowing of a trumpet signified the entrance of the king and his retinue. The annual Feast of Trumpets therefore rightly symbolizes the return of Yeshua as conquering King. It would be consistent with the biblical pattern for the seven trumpets to cover a seven-year period—one year for each Feast of Trumpets. The time frame in the Book of Revelation speeds up as the judgments come closer to an end.

Seven bowls follow the seven trumpets. This is the most intense time of wrath and warfare. The final conflict between God and the nations comes to a head. The seven bowls of wrath take place in a relatively short period of time. The Feast of Trumpets takes place on the first day of the seventh month. The Day of Atonement takes place on the tenth day. If the seventh trumpet of Revelation is blown on the Feast of Trumpets and the Day of Atonement trumpet announces the start of the Jubilee Age, there are approximately ten days in which those cataclysmic events of final judgment will take place. It is interesting that the Jewish rabbis refer to the ten days between Rosh Hashanah and Yom Kippur as "The Ten Days of Awe." Remember the events surrounding the Crucifixion and Resurrection of Yeshua all took place in the same year on the exact days of the feasts foreshadowing them.

We will better understand the timing of events in the Book of Revelation if we recognize that the seven seals cover an extended period of time leading up to the final conflicts, the seven trumpets take place during the span of seven yearly Feasts of Trumpets, and the seven bowls of wrath will be fulfilled rapidly in the last year of this present age.

About Dan Juster
and Tikkun Ministries

Dr. Daniel Juster is the Director of Tikkun International, a network of congregations and ministries in the United States and abroad. He was an honors graduate in philosophy from Wheaton College, completed graduate course work for a degree in Philosophy of Religion at Trinity Evangelical Seminary, and received a Masters of Divinity from McCormick Theological Seminary. He also received a Th. D. from New Covenant International Seminary, New Zealand.

Founding president of the Union of Messianic Jewish Congregations, which he served as president and general secretary, he also pastored congregations *Adat Hatikvah* in Chicago and later *Beth Messiah* in suburban Washington, D.C. from 1978-2000. In recent years, he and his wife Patty have resided near Jerusalem.

Dr. Juster is an author of several books on Messianic Jewish theology and apologetics. He serves on numerous boards to further the Messianic Jewish movement and the Church.

Tikkun International is the U.S. agency for Revive Israel and Ohalai Rachamim, which are planting, discipleship, and networking ministries in Israel. Tikkun also provides oversight of the international teaching and networking ministry of Dr. Juster. Tikkun America, a part of Tikkun International, links a network of Messianic Jewish Congregations in North America.

His ministry may be contacted at
www.**Tikkunministries.org**,
or by writing Tikkun@tikkunministries.org.

They are desirous of expanding
partnership for the salvation of Israel.

OTHER RELATED RESOURCES

Complete Jewish Bible: *A New English Version*
—Dr. David H. Stern

Presenting the Word of God as a unified Jewish book, the *Complete Jewish Bible* is a new version for Jews and non-Jews alike. It connects Jews with the Jewishness of the Messiah, and non-Jews with their Jewish roots. Names and key terms are returned to their original Hebrew and presented in easy-to-understand transliterations, enabling the reader to say them the way Yeshua (Jesus) did! 1697 pages.

Hardback	978-9653590151	**JB12**	$34.99
Paperback	978-9653590182	**JB13**	$29.99
Leather Cover	978-9653590199	**JB15**	$59.99
Large Print (12 Pt font)	978-1880226483	**JB16**	$49.99

Also available in French and Portuguese.

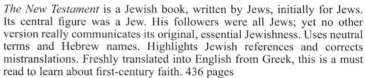

Jewish New Testament
—Dr. David H. Stern

The New Testament is a Jewish book, written by Jews, initially for Jews. Its central figure was a Jew. His followers were all Jews; yet no other version really communicates its original, essential Jewishness. Uses neutral terms and Hebrew names. Highlights Jewish references and corrects mistranslations. Freshly translated into English from Greek, this is a must read to learn about first-century faith. 436 pages

Hardback	978-9653590069	**JB02**	$19.99
Paperback	978-9653590038	**JB01**	$14.99
Spanish	978-1936716272	**JB17**	$24.99

Also available in French, German, Polish, Portuguese and Russian.

Jewish New Testament Commentary
—Dr. David H. Stern

This companion to the *Jewish New Testament* enhances Bible study. Passages and expressions are explained in their original cultural context. 15 years of research. 960 pages.

Hardback	978-9653590083	**JB06**	$34.99
Paperback	978-9653590113	**JB10**	$29.99

Psalms & Proverbs *Tehillim* תְּהִלִּים-*Mishlei* מִשְׁלֵי
—Translated by Dr. David Stern

Contemplate the power in these words anytime, anywhere: Psalms-*Tehillim* offers uplifting words of praise and gratitude, keeping us focused with the right attitude; Proverbs-*Mishlei* gives us the wisdom for daily living, renewing our minds by leading us to examine our actions, to discern good from evil, and to decide freely to do the good. Makes a wonderful and meaningful gift. Softcover, 224 pages.

978-1936716692	LB90	$9.99

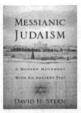

Messianic Judaism *A Modern Movement With an Ancient Past*
—David H. Stern

An updated discussion of the history, ideology, theology and program for Messianic Judaism. A challenge to both Jews and non-Jews who honor Yeshua to catch the vision of Messianic Judaism. 312 pages

978-1880226339 **LB62** $17.99

Restoring the Jewishness of the Gospel
A Message for Christians
—David H. Stern

Introduces Christians to the Jewish roots of their faith, challenges some conventional ideas, and raises some neglected questions: How are both the Jews and "the Church" God's people? Is the Law of Moses in force today? Filled with insight! Endorsed by Dr. Darrell L. Bock. 110 pages

English	978-1880226667	**LB70**	$9.99
Spanish	978-9653590175	**JB14**	$9.99

Come and Worship *Ways to Worship from the Hebrew Scriptures*
—Compiled by Barbara D. Malda

We were created to worship. God has graciously given us many ways to express our praise to him. Each way fits a different situation or moment in life, yet all are intended to bring honor and glory to him. When we believe that he is who he says he is [see *His Names are Wonderful!*] and that his Word is true, worship flows naturally from our hearts to his. Softcover, 128 pages.

978-1936716678 **LB88** $9.99

His Names Are Wonderful
Getting to Know God Through His Hebrew Names
—Elizabeth L. Vander Meulen and Barbara D. Malda

In Hebrew thought, names did more than identify people; they revealed their nature. God's identity is expressed not in one name, but in many. This book will help readers know God better as they uncover the truths in his Hebrew names. 160 pages.

978-1880226308 **LB58** $9.99

The Return of the Kosher Pig *The Divine Messiah in Jewish Thought*
—Rabbi Tzahi Shapira

The subject of Messiah fills many pages of rabbinic writings. Hidden in those pages is a little known concept that the Messiah has the same authority given to God. Based on the Scriptures and traditional rabbinic writings, this book shows the deity of Yeshua from a new perspective. You will see that the rabbis of old expected the Messiah to be divine. Softcover, 352 pages.

"One of the most interesting and learned tomes I have ever read. Contained within its pages is much with which I agree, some with which I disagree, and much about which I never thought. Rabbi Shapria's remarkable book cannot be ignored."

—Dr. Paige Patterson, President, Southwest Baptist Theological Seminary

978-1936716456 **LB81** $ 39.99

Matthew Presents Yeshua, King Messiah *A Messianic Commentary*
—Rabbi Barney Kasdan

Few commentators are able to truly present Yeshua in his Jewish context. Most don't understand his background, his family, even his religion, and consequently really don't understand who he truly is. This commentator is well versed with first-century Jewish practices and thought, as well as the historical and cultural setting of the day, and the 'traditions of the Elders' that Yeshua so often spoke about. Get to know Yeshua, the King, through the writing of another rabbi, Barney Kasdan. 448 pages

978-1936716265 **LB76** $29.99

James the Just Presents Application of Torah
A Messianic Commentary
—Dr. David Friedman

James (Jacob) one of the Epistles written to first century Jewish followers of Yeshua. Dr. David Friedman, a former Professor of the Israel Bible Institute has shed new light for Christians from this very important letter.

978-1936716449 **LB82** $14.99

Jude On Faith and the Destructive Influence of Heresy
A Messianic Commentary
—Rabbi Joshua Brumbach

Almost no other canonical book has been as neglected and overlooked as the Epistle of Jude. This little book may be small, but it has a big message that is even more relevant today as when it was originally written.

978-1-936716-78-4 **LB97** $14.99

Conveying Our Heritage A Messianic Jewish Guide to Home Practice
—Daniel C. Juster, Th.D. Patricia A. Juster

Throughout history the heritage of faith has been conveyed within the family and the congregation. The first institution in the Bible is the family and only the family can raise children with an adequate appreciation of our faith and heritage. This guide exists to help families learn how to pass on the heritage of spiritual Messianic Jewish life. Softcover, 86 pages

978-1936716739 **LB93** $8.99

Mutual Blessing *Discovering the Ultimate Destiny of Creation*
—Daniel C. Juster

To truly love as God loves is to see the wonder and richness of the distinct differences in all of creation and his natural order of interdependence. This is the way to mutual blessing and the discovery of the ultimate destiny of creation. Learn how to become enriched and blessed as you enrich and bless others and all that is around you! Softcover, 135 pages.

978-1936716746 **LB94** $9.99

At the Feet of Rabbi Gamaliel
Rabbinic Influence in Paul's Teachings
—David Friedman, Ph.D.

Paul (Shaul) was on the "fast track" to becoming a sage and Sanhedrin judge, describing himself as passionate for the Torah and the traditions of the fathers, typical for an aspiring Pharisee: "...trained at the feet of Gamaliel in every detail of the Torah of our forefathers. I was a zealot for God, as all of you are today" (Acts 22.3, CJB). Did Shaul's teachings reflect Rabbi Gamaliel's instructions? Did Paul continue to value the Torah and Pharisaic tradition? Did Paul create a 'New' Theology? The results of the research within these pages and its conclusion may surprise you. Softcover, 100 pages.

978-1936716753   **LB95** $8.99

Debranding God *Revealing His True Essence*
—Eduardo Stein

The process of 'debranding' God is to remove all the labels and fads that prompt us to understand him as a supplier and ourselves as the most demanding of customers. Changing our perception of God also changes our perception of ourselves. In knowing who we are in relationship to God, we discover his, and our, true essence. Softcover, 252 pages.

978-1936716708   **LB91** $16.99

Under the Fig Tree *Messianic Thought Through the Hebrew Calendar*
—Patrick Gabriel Lumbroso

Take a daily devotional journey into the Word of God through the Hebrew Calendar and the Biblical Feasts. Learn deeper meaning of the Scriptures through Hebraic thought. Beautifully written and a source for inspiration to draw closer to Adonai every day. Softcover, 407 pages.

978-1936716760   **LB96** $25.99

Under the Vine *Messianic Thought Through the Hebrew Calendar*
—Patrick Gabriel Lumbroso

Journey daily through the Hebrew Calendar and Biblical Feasts into the B'rit Hadashah (New Testament) Scriptures as they are put in their rightful context, bringing Judaism alive in it's full beauty. Messianic faith was the motor and what gave substance to Abraham's new beliefs, hope to Job, trust to Isaac, vision to Jacob, resilience to Joseph, courage to David, wisdom to Solomon, knowledge to Daniel, and divine Messianic authority to Yeshua. Softcover, 412 pages.

978-1936716654   **LB87** $25.99

The Revolt of Rabbi Morris Cohen
Exploring the Passion & Piety of a Modern-day Pharisee
—Anthony Cardinale

A brilliant school psychologist, Rabbi Morris Cohen went on a one-man strike to protest the systematic mislabeling of slow learning pupils as "Learning Disabled" (to extract special education money from the state). His disciplinary hearing, based on the transcript, is a hilarious read! This effusive, garrulous man with an irresistible sense of humor lost his job, but achieved a major historic victory causing the reform of the billion-dollar special education program. Enter into the mind of an eighth-generation Orthodox rabbi to see how he deals spiritually with the loss of everything, even the love of his children. This modern-day Pharisee discovered a trusted friend in the author (a born again believer in Jesus) with whom he could openly struggle over Rabbinic Judaism as well as the concept of Jesus (Yeshua) as Messiah. Softcover, 320 pages.

978-1936716722 **LB92** $19.99

Stories of Yeshua
—Jim Reimann, Illustrator Julia Filipone-Erez

Children's Bible Storybook with four stories about Yeshua (Jesus).
Yeshua is Born: The Bethlehem Story based on Lk 1:26-35 & 2:1-20; *Yeshua and Nicodemus in Jerusalem* based on Jn 3:1-16; *Yeshua Loves the Little Children of the World* based on Matthew 18:1–6 & 19:13–15; *Yeshua is Alive-The Empty Tomb in Jerusalem* based on Matthew 26:17-56, Jn 19:16-20:18, Lk 24:50-53. Ages 3-7, Softcover, 48 pages.

978-1936716685 **LB89** $14.99

To the Ends of the Earth – How the First Jewish Followers of Yeshua Transformed the Ancient World
— Dr. Jeffrey Seif

Everyone knows that the first followers of Yeshua were Jews, and that Christianity was very Jewish for the first 50 to 100 years. It's a known fact that there were many congregations made up mostly of Jews, although the false perception today is, that in the second century they disappeared. Dr. Seif reveals the truth of what happened to them and how these early Messianic Jews influenced and transformed the behavior of the known world at that time.

978-1936716463 **LB83** $17.99

Passion for Israel: *A Short History of the Evangelical Church's Support of Israel and the Jewish People*
—Dan Juster

History reveals a special commitment of Christians to the Jews as God's still elect people, but the terrible atrocities committed against the Jews by so-called Christians have overshadowed the many good deeds that have been performed. This important history needs to be told to help heal the wounds and to inspire more Christians to stand together in support of Israel.

978-1936716401 **LB78** $9.99

Jewish Roots and Foundations of the Scriptures I
—John Fischer, Th.D, Ph.D.

An outstanding evangelical leader once said: "There is something shallow about a Christianity that has lost its Jewish roots." A beautiful painting is a careful interweaving of a number of elements. Among other things, there are the background, the foreground and the subject. Discovering the roots of your faith is a little like appreciating the various parts of a painting. In the background is the panorama of preparation and pictures found in the Old Testament. In the foreground is the landscape and light of the first century Jewish setting. All of this is intricately connected with and highlights the subject—which becomes the flowering of all these aspects—the coming of God to earth and what that means for us. Discovering and appreciating your roots in this way broadens, deepens and enriches your faith and your understanding of Scripture. This audio is 32 hours of live class instruction - audio is clear and easy to understand.

9781936716623   **LCD03** $49.99

The Gospels in their Jewish Context
—John Fischer, Th.D, Ph.D.

An examination of the Jewish background and nature of the Gospels in their contemporary political, cultural and historical settings, emphasizing each gospel's special literary presentation of Yeshua, and highlighting the cultural and religious contexts necessary for understanding each of the gospels. 32 hours of audio/video instruction on MP3-DVD and pdf of syllabus.

978-1936716241   **LCD01** $49.99

The Epistles from a Jewish Perspective
—John Fischer, Th.D, Ph.D.

An examination of the relationship of Rabbi Shaul (the Apostle Paul) and the Apostles to their Jewish contemporaries and environment; surveys their Jewish practices, teaching, controversy with the religious leaders, and many critical passages, with emphasis on the Jewish nature, content, and background of these letters. 32 hours of audio/video instruction on MP3-DVD and pdf of syllabus.

978-1936716258   **LCD02** $49.99

The Red Heifer *A Jewish Cry for Messiah*
—Anthony Cardinale

Award-winning journalist and playwright Anthony Cardinale has traveled extensively in Israel, and recounts here his interviews with Orthodox rabbis, secular Israelis, and Palestinian Arabs about the current search for a red heifer by Jewish radicals wishing to rebuild the Temple and bring the Messiah. These real-life interviews are interwoven within an engaging and dramatic fictional portrayal of the diverse people of Israel and how they would react should that red heifer be found. Readers will find themselves in the Land, where they can hear learned rabbis and ordinary Israelis talking about the red heifer and dealing with all the related issues and the imminent coming and identity of Messiah.

978-1936716470   LB79 $19.99

The Borough Park Papers
—Multiple Authors

As you read the New Testament, you "overhear" debates first-century Messianic Jews had about critical issues, e.g. Gentiles being "allowed" into the Messianic kingdom (Acts 15). Similarly, you're now invited to "listen in" as leading twenty-first century Messianic Jewish theologians discuss critical issues facing us today. Some ideas may not fit into your previously held pre-suppositions or pre-conceptions. Indeed, you may find some paradigm shifting in your thinking. We want to share the thoughts of these thinkers with you, our family in the Messiah.

Symposium I:
The Gospel and the Jewish People
248 pages

978-1936716593	LB84	$39.95

Symposium II:
The Deity of Messiah and the Mystery of God
211 pages

978-1936716609	LB85	$39.95

Symposium III:
How Jewish Should the Messianic Community Be?

978-1936716616	LB86	$39.95

On The Way to Emmaus: *Searching the Messianic Prophecies*
—Dr. Jacques Doukhan

An outstanding compilation of the most critical Messianic prophecies by a renowned conservative Christian Scholar, drawing on material from the Bible, Rabbinic sources, Dead Sea Scrolls, and more.

978-1936716432	LB80	$14.99

Yeshua *A Guide to the Real Jesus and the Original Church*
—Dr. Ron Moseley

Opens up the history of the Jewish roots of the Christian faith. Illuminates the Jewish background of Yeshua and the Church and never flinches from showing "Jesus was a Jew, who was born, lived, and died, within first century Judaism." Explains idioms in the New Testament. Endorsed by Dr. Brad Young and Dr. Marvin Wilson. 213 pages.

978-1880226681	**LB29**	$12.99

Gateways to Torah *Joining the Ancient Conversation on the Weekly Portion*
—Rabbi Russell Resnik

From before the days of Messiah until today, Jewish people have read from and discussed a prescribed portion of the Pentateuch each week. Now, a Messianic Jewish Rabbi, Russell Resnik, brings another perspective on the Torah, that of a Messianic Jew. 246 pages.

978-1880226889   **LB42** $15.99

Creation to Completion *A Guide to Life's Journey from the Five Books of Moses*
—Rabbi Russell Resnik

Endorsed by Coach Bill McCartney, Founder of Promise Keepers & Road to Jerusalem: "Paul urged Timothy to study the Scriptures (2 Tim. 3:16), advising him to apply its teachings to all aspects of his life. Since there was no New Testament then, this rabbi/apostle was convinced that his disciple would profit from studying the Torah, the Five Books of Moses, and the Old Testament. Now, Rabbi Resnik has written a warm devotional commentary that will help you understand and apply the Law of Moses to your life in a practical way." 256 pages

978-1880226322   **LB61** $14.99

Walk Genesis! Walk Exodus! Walk Leviticus! Walk Numbers! Walk Deuteronomy!
Messianic Jewish Devotional Commentaries
—Jeffrey Enoch Feinberg, Ph.D.

Using the weekly synagogue readings, Dr. Jeffrey Feinberg has put together some very valuable material in his "Walk" series. Each section includes a short Hebrew lesson (for the non-Hebrew speaker), key concepts, an excellent overview of the portion, and some practical applications. Can be used as a daily devotional as well as a Bible study tool.

Walk Genesis!	238 pages	978-1880226759	**LB34**	$12.99
Walk Exodus!	224 pages	978-1880226872	**LB40**	$12.99
Walk Leviticus!	208 pages	978-1880226926	**LB45**	$12.99
Walk Numbers!	211 pages	978-1880226995	**LB48**	$12.99
Walk Deuteronomy!	231 pages	978-1880226186	**LB51**	$12.99
SPECIAL! Five-book Walk!		5 Book Set **Save $10**	**LK28**	$54.99

Good News According To Matthew
—Dr. Henry Einspruch

English translation with quotations from the Tanakh (Old Testament) capitalized and printed in Hebrew. Helpful notations are included. Lovely black and white illustrations throughout the book. 86 pages.

| | 978-1880226025 | **LB03** | $4.99 |
| Also available in Yiddish. | | **LB02** | $4.99 |

They Loved the Torah *What Yeshua's First Followers Really Thought About the Law*
—Dr. David Friedman

Although many Jews believe that Paul taught against the Law, this book disproves that notion. An excellent case for his premise that all the first followers of the Messiah were not only Torah-observant, but also desired to spread their love for God's entire Word to the gentiles to whom they preached. 144 pages. Endorsed by Dr. David Stern, Ariel Berkowitz, Rabbi Dr. Stuart Dauermann & Dr. John Fischer.

978-1880226940   **LB47** $9.99

The Distortion *2000 Years of Misrepresenting the Relationship Between Jesus the Messiah and the Jewish People*
—Dr. John Fischer & Dr. Patrice Fischer

Did the Jews kill Jesus? Did they really reject him? With the rise of global anti–Semitism, it is important to understand what the Gospels teach about the relationship between Jewish people and their Messiah. 2000 years of distortion have made this difficult. Learn how the distortion began and continues to this day and what you can do to change it. 126 pages. Endorsed by Dr. Ruth Fleischer, Rabbi Russell Resnik, Dr. Daniel C. Juster, Dr. Michael Rydelnik.

978-1880226254   **LB54** $11.99

---

eBooks Now Available!
All books are available as ebooks
for your favorite reader

Visit www.messianicjewish.net for direct links to these readers for each available eBook.

God's Appointed Times *A Practical Guide to Understanding and Celebrating the Biblical Holidays* – **New Edition.**

—Rabbi Barney Kasdan

The Biblical Holy Days teach us about the nature of God and his plan for mankind, and can be a source of God's blessing for all believers–Jews and Gentiles–today. Includes historical background, traditional Jewish observance, New Testament relevance, and prophetic significance, plus music, crafts and holiday recipes. 145 pages.

English	978-1880226353	**LB63**	$12.99
Spanish	978-1880226391	**LB59**	$12.99

God's Appointed Customs *A Messianic Jewish Guide to the Biblical Lifecycle and Lifestyle*

— Rabbi Barney Kasdan

Explains how biblical customs are often the missing key to unlocking the depths of Scripture. Discusses circumcision, the Jewish wedding, and many more customs mentioned in the New Testament. Companion to *God's Appointed Times*. 170 pages.

English	978-1880226636	**LB26**	$12.99
Spanish	978-1880226551	**LB60**	$12.99

Celebrations of the Bible *A Messianic Children's Curriculum*

Did you know that each Old Testament feast or festival finds its fulfillment in the New? They enrich the lives of people who experience and enjoy them. Our popular curriculum for children is in a brand new, user-friendly format. The lay-flat at binding allows you to easily reproduce handouts and worksheets. Celebrations of the Bible has been used by congregations, Sunday schools, ministries, homeschoolers, and individuals to teach children about the biblical festivals. Each of these holidays are presented for Preschool (2-K), Primary (Grades 1-3), Junior (Grades 4-6), and Children's Worship/Special Services. 208 pages.

978-1880226261	**LB55**	$24.99

Passover: *The Key That Unlocks the Book of Revelation*

—Daniel C. Juster, Th.D.

Is there any more enigmatic book of the Bible than Revelation? Controversy concerning its meaning has surrounded it back to the first century. Today, the arguments continue. Yet, Dan Juster has given us the key that unlocks the entire book—the events and circumstances of the Passover/Exodus. By interpreting Revelation through the lens of Exodus, Dan Juster provides a unified overview that helps us read Revelation as it was always meant to be read, as a drama of spiritual conflict, deliverance, and above all, worship. He also shows how this final drama, fulfilled in Messiah, resonates with the Torah and all of God's Word. — Russ Resnik, Executive Director, Union of Messianic Jewish Congregations.

978-1936716210	**LB74**	$10.99

The Messianic Passover Haggadah
Revised and Updated
—Rabbi Barry Rubin and Steffi Rubin.

Guides you through the traditional Passover seder dinner, step-by-step. Not only does this observance remind us of our rescue from Egyptian bondage, but, we remember Messiah's last supper, a Passover seder. The theme of redemption is seen throughout the evening. What's so unique about our Haggadah is the focus on Yeshua (Jesus) the Messiah and his teaching, especially on his last night in the upper room. 36 pages.

English	978-1880226292	**LB57**	$4.99
Spanish	978-1880226599	**LBSP01**	$4.99

The Messianic Passover Seder Preparation Guide
Includes recipes, blessings and songs. 19 pages.

English	978-1880226247	**LB10**	$2.99
Spanish	978-1880226728	**LBSP02**	$2.99

The Sabbath *Entering God's Rest*
—Barry Rubin & Steffi Rubin

Even if you've never celebrated Shabbat before, this book will guide you into the rest God has for all who would enter in—Jews and non-Jews. Contains prayers, music, recipes; in short, everything you need to enjoy the Sabbath, even how to observe havdalah, the closing ceremony of the Sabbath. Also discusses the Saturday or Sunday controversy. 48 pages.

978-1880226742   **LB32** $6.99

Havdalah *The Ceremony that Completes the Sabbath*
—Dr. Neal & Jamie Lash

The Sabbath ends with this short, yet equally sweet ceremony called havdalah (separation). This ceremony reminds us to be a light and a sweet fragrance in this world of darkness as we carry the peace, rest, joy and love of the Sabbath into the work week. 28 pages.

978-1880226605   **LB69** $4.99

Dedicate and Celebrate!
A Messianic Jewish Guide to Hanukkah
—Barry Rubin & Family

Hanukkah means "dedication" — a theme of significance for Jews and Christians. Discussing its historical background, its modern-day customs, deep meaning for all of God's people, this little book covers all the how-tos! Recipes, music, and prayers for lighting the menorah, all included! 32 pages.

978-1880226834   **LB36** $4.99

The Conversation
An Intimate Journal of the Emmaus Encounter
—Judy Salisbury

"Then beginning with Moses and with all the prophets, He explained to them the things concerning Himself in all the Scriptures." Luke 24:27
If you've ever wondered what that conversation must have been like, this captivating book takes you there.

"The Conversation brings to life that famous encounter between the two disciples and our Lord Jesus on the road to Emmaus. While it is based in part on an imaginative reconstruction, it is filled with the throbbing pulse of the excitement of the sensational impact that our Lord's resurrection should have on all of our lives." ~ Dr. Walter Kaiser President Emeritus Gordon-Conwell Theological Seminary. Hardcover 120 pages.

Hardcover	978-1936716173	**LB73**	$14.99
Paperback	978-1936716364	**LB77**	$9.99

Growing to Maturity
A Messianic Jewish Discipleship Guide
—Daniel C. Juster, Th.D.

This discipleship series presents first steps of understanding and spiritual practice, tailored for the Jewish believer. It's purpose is to aid the believer in living according to Yeshua's will as a disciple, one who has learned the example of his teacher. The course is structured according to recent advances in individualized educational instruction. Discipleship is serious business and the material is geared for serious study and reflection. Each chapter is divided into short sections followed by study questions. 256 pages.

978-1936716227	**LB75**	$19.99

Growing to Maturity Primer: *A Messianic Jewish Discipleship Workbook*
—Daniel C. Juster, Th.D.

A basic book of material in question and answer form. Usable by everyone. 60 pages.

978-0961455507	**TB16**	$7.99

Proverbial Wisdom & Common Sense
—Derek Leman

A Messianic Jewish Approach to Today's Issues from the Proverbs Unique in style and scope, this commentary on the book of Proverbs, written in devotional style, is divided into chapters suitable for daily reading. A virtual encyclopedia of practical advice on family, sex, finances, gossip, honesty, love, humility, and discipline. Endorsed by Dr. John Walton, Dr. Jeffrey Feinberg and Rabbi Barney Kasdan. 248 pages.

978-1880226780	**LB35**	$14.99

That They May Be One *A Brief Review of Church Restoration Movements and Their Connection to the Jewish People*
—Daniel Juster, Th.D

Something prophetic and momentous is happening. The Church is finally fully grasping its relationship to Israel and the Jewish people. Author describes the restoration movements in Church history and how they connected to Israel and the Jewish people. Each one contributed in some way—some more, some less—toward the ultimate unity between Jews and Gentiles. Predicted in the Old Testament and fulfilled in the New, Juster believes this plan of God finds its full expression in Messianic Judaism. He may be right. See what you think as you read *That They May Be One.* 100 pages.

978-1880226711   **LB71** $9.99

The Greatest Commandment
How the Sh'ma Leads to More Love in Your Life
—Irene Lipson

"What is the greatest commandment?" Yeshua was asked. His reply—"Hear, O Israel, the Lord our God, the Lord is one, and you are to love Adonai your God with all your heart, with all your soul, with all your understanding, and all your strength." A superb book explaining each word so the meaning can be fully grasped and lived. Endorsed by Elliot Klayman, Susan Perlman, & Robert Stearns. 175 pages.

978-1880226360   **LB65** $12.99

Blessing the King of the Universe
Transforming Your Life Through the Practice of Biblical Praise
—Irene Lipson

Insights into the ancient biblical practice of blessing God are offered clearly and practically. With examples from Scripture and Jewish tradition, this book teaches the biblical formula used by men and women of the Bible, including the Messiah; points to new ways and reasons to praise the Lord; and explains more about the Jewish roots of the faith. Endorsed by Rabbi Barney Kasdan, Dr. Mitch Glaser, & Rabbi Dr. Dan Cohn-Sherbok. 144 pages.

978-1880226797   **LB53** $11.99

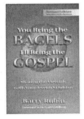

You Bring the Bagels, I'll Bring the Gospel
Sharing the Messiah with Your Jewish Neighbor
Revised Edition—Now with Study Questions
—Rabbi Barry Rubin

This "how-to-witness-to-Jewish-people" book is an orderly presentation of everything you need to share the Messiah with a Jewish friend. Includes Messianic prophecies, Jewish objections to believing, sensitivities in your witness, words to avoid. A "must read" for all who care about the Jewish people. Good for individual or group study. Used in Bible schools. Endorsed by Harold A. Sevener, Dr. Walter C. Kaiser, Dr. Erwin J. Kolb and Dr. Arthur F. Glasser. 253 pages.

English	978-1880226650	**LB13**	$12.99
Te Tengo Buenas Noticias	978-0829724103	**OBSP02**	$14.99

Making Eye Contact With God
A Weekly Devotional for Women
—Terri Gillespie

What kind of eyes do you have? Are they downcast and sad? Are they full of God's joy and passion? See yourself through the eyes of God. Using real life anecdotes, combined with scripture, the author reveals God's heart for women everywhere, as she softly speaks of the ways in which women see God. Endorsed by prominent authors: Dr. Angela Hunt, Wanda Dyson and Kathryn Mackel. 247 pages, hardcover.

978-1880226513 **LB68** $19.99

Divine Reversal
The Transforming Ethics of Jesus
—Rabbi Russell Resnik

In the Old Testament, God often reversed the plans of man. Yeshua's ethics continue this theme. Following his path transforms one's life from within, revealing the source of true happiness, forgiveness, reconciliation, fidelity and love. From the introduction, "As a Jewish teacher, Jesus doesn't separate matters of theology from practice. His teaching is consistently practical, ethical, and applicable to real life, even two thousand years after it was originally given." Endorsed by Jonathan Bernis, Dr. Daniel C. Juster, Dr. Jeffrey L. Seif, and Dr Darrell Bock. 206 pages

978-1880226803 **LB72** $12.99

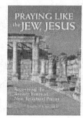

Praying Like the Jew, Jesus
Recovering the Ancient Roots of New Testament Prayer
—Dr. Timothy P. Jones

This eye-opening book reveals the Jewish background of many of Yeshua's prayers. Historical vignettes "transport" you to the times of Yeshua so you can grasp the full meaning of Messiah's prayers. Unique devotional thoughts and meditations, presented in down-to-earth language, provide inspiration for a more meaningful prayer life and help you draw closer to God. Endorsed by Mark Galli, James W. Goll, Rev. Robert Stearns, James F. Strange, and Dr. John Fischer. 144 pages.

978-1880226285 **LB56** $9.99

Growing Your Olive Tree Marriage *A Guide for Couples from Two Traditions*
—David J. Rudolph

One partner is Jewish; the other is Christian. Do they celebrate Hanukkah, Christmas or both? Do they worship in a church or a synagogue? How will the children be raised? This is the first book from a biblical perspective that addresses the concerns of intermarried couples, offering a godly solution. Includes highlights of interviews with intermarried couples. Endorsed by Walter C. Kaiser, Jr., Rabbi Dan Cohn-Sherbok, Jonathan Settel, Dr. Mitchell Glaser & Natalie Sirota. 224 pages.

978-1880226179 **LB50** $12.99

In Search of the Silver Lining *Where is God in the Midst of Life's Storms?*
—Jerry Gramckow

When faced with suffering, what are your choices? Storms have always raged. And people have either perished in their wake or risen above the tempests, shaping history by their responses...new storms are on the horizon. How will we deal with them? How will we shape history or those who follow us? The answer lies in how we view God in the midst of the storms. Endorsed by Joseph C. Aldrich, Ray Beeson, Dr. Daniel Juster. 176 pages.

978-1880226865 **LB39** $10.99

The Voice of the Lord *Messianic Jewish Daily Devotional*
—Edited by David J. Rudolph

Brings insight into the Jewish Scriptures—both Old and New Testaments. Twenty-two prominent Messianic contributors provide practical ways to apply biblical truth. Start your day with this unique resource. Explanatory notes. Perfect companion to the Complete Jewish Bible (see page 2). Endorsed by Edith Schaeffer, Dr. Arthur F. Glaser, Dr. Michael L. Brown, Mitch Glaser and Moishe Rosen. 416 pages.

9781880226704 **LB31** $19.99

Kingdom Relationships *God's Laws for the Community of Faith*
—Dr. Ron Moseley

Dr. Ron Moseley's Yeshua: A Guide to the Real Jesus and the Original Church has taught thousands of people about the Jewishness of not only Yeshua, but of the first followers of the Messiah.

In this work, Moseley focuses on the teaching of Torah -- the Five Books of Moses -- tapping into truths that greatly help modern-day members of the community of faith.

The first section explains the relationship of both the Jewish people and Christians to the Kingdom of God. The second section lists the laws that are applicable to a non-Jew living in the twenty-first century and outside of the land of Israel.

This book is needed because these little known laws of God's Kingdom were, according to Yeshua, the most salient features of the first-century community of believers. Yeshua even warned that anyone breaking these laws would be least in the Kingdom (Matt. 5:19). Additionally, these laws will be the basis for judgment at the end of every believer's life. 64 pages.

978-1880226841 **LB37** $8.99

Train Up A Child *Successful Parenting For The Next Generation*
—Dr. Daniel L. Switzer

The author, former principal of Ets Chaiyim Messianic Jewish Day School, and father of four, combines solid biblical teaching with Jewish sources on child raising, focusing on the biblical holy days, giving fresh insight into fulfilling the role of parent. 188 pages. Endorsed by Dr. David J. Rudolph, Paul Lieberman, and Dr. David H. Stern.

978-1880226377 **LB64** $12.99

Fire on the Mountain - *Past Renewals, Present Revivals and the Coming Return of Israel*
—Dr. Louis Goldberg

The term "revival" is often used to describe a person or congregation turning to God. Is this something that "just happens," or can it be brought about? Dr. Louis Goldberg, author and former professor of Hebrew and Jewish Studies at Moody Bible Institute, examines real revivals that took place in Bible times and applies them to today. 268 pages.

978-1880226858   **LB38** $15.99

Voices of Messianic Judaism *Confronting Critical Issues Facing a Maturing Movement*
—General Editor Rabbi Dan Cohn-Sherbok

Many of the best minds of the Messianic Jewish movement contributed their thoughts to this collection of 29 substantive articles. Challenging questions are debated: The involvement of Gentiles in Messianic Judaism? How should outreach be accomplished? Liturgy or not? Intermarriage? 256 pages.

978-1880226933   **LB46** $15.99

The Enduring Paradox *Exploratory Essays in Messianic Judaism*
—General Editor Dr. John Fischer

Yeshua and his Jewish followers began a new movement—Messianic Judaism—2,000 years ago. In the 20th century, it was reborn. Now, at the beginning of the 21st century, it is maturing. Twelve essays from top contributors to the theology of this vital movement of God, including: Dr. Walter C. Kaiser, Dr. David H. Stern, and Dr. John Fischer. 196 pages.

978-1880226902   **LB43** $13.99

The World To Come *A Portal to Heaven on Earth*
—Derek Leman

An insightful book, exposing fallacies and false teachings surrounding this extremely important subject... paints a hopeful picture of the future and dispels many non-biblical notions. Intriguing chapters: Magic and Desire, The Vision of the Prophets, Hints of Heaven, Horrors of Hell, The Drama of the Coming Ages. Offers a fresh, but old, perspective on the world to come, as it interacts with the prophets of Israel and the Bible. 110 pages.

978-1880226049   **LB67**   .$9.99

Hebrews Through a Hebrew's Eyes
—Dr. Stuart Sacks

Written to first-century Messianic Jews, this epistle, understood through Jewish eyes, edifies and encourages all. 119 pages. Endorsed by Dr. R.C. Sproul and James M. Boice.

978-1880226612   **LB23** $10.99

The Irrevocable Calling *Israel's Role As A Light To The Nations*
—Daniel C. Juster, Th.D.

Referring to the chosen-ness of the Jewish people, Paul, the Apostle, wrote "For God's free gifts and his calling are irrevocable" (Rom. 11:29). This messenger to the Gentiles understood the unique calling of his people, Israel. So does Dr. Daniel Juster, President of Tikkun Ministries Int'l. In *The Irrevocable Calling*, he expands Paul's words, showing how Israel was uniquely chosen to bless the world and how these blessings can be enjoyed today. Endorsed by Dr. Jack Hayford, Mike Bickle and Don Finto. 64 pages.

978-1880226346   **LB66** $8.99

Are There Two Ways of Atonement?
—Dr. Louis Goldberg

Here Dr. Louis Goldberg, long-time professor of Jewish Studies at Moody Bible Institute, exposes the dangerous doctrine of Two-Covenant Theology. 32 pages.

978-1880226056   **LB12** $ 4.99

Awakening *Articles and Stories About Jews and Yeshua*
—Arranged by Anna Portnov

Articles, testimonies, and stories about Jewish people and their relationship with God, Israel, and the Messiah. Includes the effective tract, "The Most Famous Jew of All." One of our best anthologies for witnessing to Jewish people. Let this book witness for you! Russian version also available. 110 pages.

English	978-1880226094	**LB15**	$ 6.99
Russian	978-1880226018	**LB14**	$ 6.99

The Unpromised Land *The Struggle of Messianic Jews* *Gary and Shirley Beresford*
—Linda Alexander

They felt God calling them to live in Israel, the Promised Land. Wanting nothing more than to live quietly and grow old together in the country of refuge for all Jewish people, little did they suspect what events would follow to try their faith. The fight to make *aliyah*, to claim their rightful inheritance in the Promised Land, became a battle waged not only for themselves, but also for Messianic Jews all over the world that wish to return to the Jewish homeland. Here is the true saga of the Beresford's journey to the land of their forefathers. 216 pages.

978-1880226568   **LB19** $ 9.99

Death of Messiah *Twenty fascinating articles that address a subject of grief, hope, and ultimate triumph.*
—Edited by Kai Kjaer-Hansen

This compilation, written by well-known Jewish believers, addresses the issue of Messiah and offers proof that Yeshua—the true Messiah—not only died, but also was resurrected! 160 pages.

978-1880226582   **LB20** $ 8.99

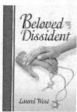

Beloved Dissident *(A Novel)*
—Laurel West

A gripping story of human relationships, passionate love, faith, and spiritual testing. Set in the world of high finance, intrigue, and international terrorism, the lives of David, Jonathan, and Leah intermingle on many levels--especially their relationships with one another and with God. As the two men tangle with each other in a rising whirlwind of excitement and danger, each hopes to win the fight for Leah's love. One of these rivals will move Leah to a level of commitment and love she has never imagined--or dared to dream. Whom will she choose? 256 pages.

978-1880226766   **LB33** $ 9.99

Sudden Terror
—Dr. David Friedman

Exposes the hidden agenda of militant Islam. The author, a former member of the Israel Defense Forces, provides eye-opening information needed in today's dangerous world.

Dr. David Friedman recounts his experiences confronting terrorism; analyzes the biblical roots of the conflict between Israel and Islam; provides an overview of early Islam; demonstrates how the United States and Israel are bound together by a common enemy; and shows how to cope with terrorism and conquer fear. The culmination of many years of research and personal experiences. This expose will prepare you for what's to come! 160 pages.

978-1880226155   **LB49** $ 9.99

It is Good! *Growing Up in a Messianic Family*
—Steffi Rubin

Growing up in a Messianic Jewish family. Meet Tovah! Tovah (Hebrew for "Good") is growing up in a Messianic Jewish home, learning the meaning of God`s special days. Ideal for young children, it teaches the biblical holidays and celebrates faith in Yeshua. 32 pages to read & color.

978-1880226063   **LB11** $ 4.99